in Search of Vision

FINDING SIGNIFICANCE THROUGH DIFFERENCE

STEVE HANAMURA

Contents

Acknowledgements

Introduction

1. *The Journey Begins* 1

2. *Getting There* 11

3. *About Love* 25

4. *Creating A Positive Self-Image* 41

5. *Embracing Change* 51

6. *Loving, Listening, and Believing* 69

7. *Living and Working from Oneness* 83

8. *Act Like A Champion* 101

9. *Keep the Faith* 115

10. *A Call to Service* 135

Acknowledgements

Words seem inadequate to express how I feel about some special people who have supported and encouraged me throughout the writing of this book. My heartfelt thanks go to Stan Blinkhorn, The Rev. Harvey Booth, and Jean Nilsen, who believed in me when I didn't believe in myself; Don and Carol Cassetty, who helped me keep important appointments to get a loan that kept us in business in the beginning; Jennifer Sah-Loeung, who worked with dedication in our office for four years and who typed the first drafts of this book; Marsia Gunter and Karen Carnahan, who had patience and belief in me as we began the business; Dr. Steve Brown, who offered encouragement when we felt like the book would never be published; and Paul Linmann, who gave straightforward feedback about the writing itself. My wife, Becky, receives the "tenacity award" for hanging in there when I was not always the best person to be around. She has given one-hundred percent support to the book, the business, and to me.

Introduction

Blindness has become my greatest *gift*. Though in the beginning I felt it was the biggest frustration, I learned through blindness a new view of life.

When I was five years old, I was sent away by my family to the California State School for the Blind in Berkeley. At that time, it was the only place in the state where a blind child could get an education. My parents and brother lived six hours away by train in Upland, California. I went home only at Christmas and for summer break.

My friends and I at school knew we were different. Still, we wanted to become successful in life. Our measure of success was whether we could mix with sighted people. We wanted to go to college, marry a sighted person, and get jobs. We also dreamed of becoming rich and famous.

As I moved up the corporate ladder and eventually started my own company, this dream of being rich and famous became even more important. My desire had become part of a disease that is crippling America. The desire to be rich and famous is self-centered. The drive to put "I" in front of "we" is hurting all levels of society in America. Corporations sacrifice employees for a higher profit margin. We are losing our sense of community.

I feel driven by the need to build self-esteem, build community, help others belong, and to help people know and feel that they are special. We need to recognize the value of being different and yet at the same time to strive to experience delight in our points of commonness.

I continually work on surrendering my life to God. It is through allowing others to serve me that I have gained new appreciation for what it means to serve others. Profit alone should not be the motivating force in business. Service is about helping others in the process.

This book is about my journey to find a new perspective. As you read, I hope you feel as though you are having coffee with a friend. I hope you discover insights, inspiration, and points of connection with your own life.

My journey is not over but it is complete. I am learning how to deal with feelings of anger, anxiety, fear, and doubt. I can face challenges and, for the most part, understand that there is much to learn from them. The more I am in the Word and prayer the more I understand how to get through difficulties.

To be at peace, we must realize we are part of something larger than any one of us individually. The common denominator is that we can have a faith that helps all of us live though the peaks and valleys of life.

A person can live forty days and nights without food, eight days without water, four minutes without breathing, but only thirty seconds without hope. I hope you keep that in mind not only for yourself but also for the stranger on the bus, the child at school, or the manager in the office.

I hope you enjoy the book and that you find a part of your story in the journey.

> Steve Hanamura
> Beaverton, Oregon

Dedication

Lord, God our Father,

I commit this book to You. As You know, I have wanted to write a book for a long time. Admittedly, the initial reasons were fame and fortune. You have taught me that I was not ready to write the book because I needed breadth and depth of experience to accurately reflect what you would like me to say. I now know that this book is to be an extension of You speaking through me and not about me promoting myself.

I felt devastated and became discouraged in the process. Now I see that I can use the same methodology for writing a book that I do for speaking in my seminars.

I commit the writing of this book back to You for Your glory and use. The book emphasizes the power of being weak in order to gain strength. It highlights the necessity of relying on others for the common good of all people and not just the self.

I hope this book will make a difference in the lives of the people who read it. I know that putting these experiences down on paper gives me clarity of purpose and acknowledgment of what I have learned from You.

It is also a way to thank You for the many blessings You have bestowed upon me.

AMEN

CHAPTER 1

The Journey Begins

I AM SITTING ON A BUS WITH FIFTEEN 1996 Olympic Games torch runners, escorts, and officials. We runners are headed for our drop-off locations. You would expect a lot of chatter among us as we anticipate the run, but tonight, as the sun sets, there's not much interaction, and I'm feeling low.

Until now we've felt exhilarated by the planning and preparation. But now it's time for the run itself, and I am feeling a little disappointed. I will be running in Salem, Oregon — not in Atlanta, where the games are being held, or in Portland, Oregon, where I live.

As if reading my thoughts, one of the organizers begins to speak. Her voice is warm and friendly. "This is an exciting night," she says. "You are among the ten-thousand people privileged to carry the Olympic torch. When it is your turn to run, take your time. Don't feel rushed. Set your own pace." And then she adds, "Don't be surprised if something happens to you out there. You just might return transformed in some way by your experience."

The bus is now approaching the town of Salem, where we will drop off the first runner. To my left is Kit, my running coach and training partner for our weekly ten-mile runs, road races, and marathons. I can now hear the other runners and their escorts begin to engage in nervous small talk. Apparently, a crowd has gathered along the road to watch the runners and the torch pass. Sensing my mood, Kit leaves me alone. She turns to the others. A man sitting directly across from her is responding to questions about having played basketball in college.

"Yeah, I was in the NBA," he says in a rich baritone.

I perk up. "Who are you?" I ask.

"Mel Counts," he says.

"No way!" I shout in disbelief. Suddenly, I am transported back to 1968. I am sitting in my dorm listening to a Los Angeles Lakers game. Mel Counts is the post-game guest. His personality comes through the radio strong and clear. He's not only a good player, but a really nice person as well. I say a prayer that night: "Dear God, let me meet Mel Counts."

Now, twenty-eight years later, I am sitting on a bus with Mel Counts, and we are both about to carry the Olympic torch. Suddenly, I no longer feel low. I engage completely in the conversation and ask at least twenty questions in two minutes.

"What was your greatest thrill?"

"Who was your best coach?"

"What was it like to be with Wilt Chamberlain, Jerry West, and Elgin Baylor?"

He is gracious and answers my questions until we are interrupted by an Olympic official who wants all of us in the bus to introduce ourselves to one another. *("Darn," I think, "I want to talk with Mel instead.")*

Still, we begin the introductions, and I note how different we are — young and old, athletes and non-athletes, with and without disabilities. Each of us has been nominated by an organization to carry the Olympic torch. By the end of the evening, every one of us will have served as a link in passing the Olympic flame around the world.

When we stop at the capitol, spectators board the bus to get autographs. Objects are placed in my hands and I sign hats, napkins, and notebooks. I feel like a celebrity.

Suddenly, it dawns on me: Others are reacting to me in the same way I had reacted to Mel Counts. Here I am, signing autographs for a crowd of people who think I am something special. Although I am enjoying the experience, I don't feel all that special. In fact, I feel I am nothing. These people asking for my autograph are making a too big a deal out of this whole thing.

Then I get a nudge of reality. This isn't just about you stupid, I think to myself. It is about what it means to carry the torch. It is about hope and harmony. The Olympic Games symbolize the coming together of people from all round the world to celebrate their human commonality. The torch symbolizes that oneness. For a few brief moments I am part of an activity that is about becoming one with everyone in the world.

I am now able to put into perspective my desire to meet Mel Counts. It is not about meeting a celebrity, though by playing for a professional sports team, Mel Counts has accomplished something that many people can only dream about. No, the pleasure I experience in talking with him lies not in his celebrity status but in the discovery that, like me, he is a human being with wants, hopes, and questions.

Finally, it's my turn. I am the next to the last runner to be dropped off. I feel sad now because I won't see these people again.

As I step off the bus, I receive a big round of applause. Overwhelmed, I learn that nearly forty people have driven from Beaverton to Salem to watch me carry the torch. I am astounded. I have been met by friends and neighbors.

As I holler at Randy Banks, a good friend and running partner, telling him I finally met Mel Counts, an elderly woman asks if I need to hold the torch with both hands.

"No," I reply.

"Well then," she says, "may I shake your hand?"

"Sure," I say, warming to the moment.

A young mother asks if her son can touch the torch.

"You bet," I say. Though I am deeply touched by the attention and support, I am also reminded once again that this is not about me alone. It is about something much bigger. It is about hope, peace, harmony, and what we share as human beings.

A hush comes over the crowd as the lead car approaches. Kit and I walk to the road. In my left hand is the torch, which is filled with propane. An Olympic official turns on the gas. I am facing left as the runner who is to light my torch nears. Everyone can see the flame. Soon, he is next to me. He lights my torch. A big roar comes from the crowd, and I am on my way.

On my right, Kit holds one end of the bungee cord, which allows me to run freely but keeps me in a safe path. The Olympic escort runner is to my left. I can hear motorcycles on both sides. Kit tells me that there is an Atlanta police car in front as well as an Oregon State Police car and a truck transporting the media. Occasionally Kit instructs me how to hold the torch so it remains upright.

Four short minutes later it is all over.

I wait for the bus to take Kit and me back to the starting point. As I board the bus, I hear a big cheer. I get to see my fellow runners again after all! The mood is joyous. We sing many songs celebrating our experience. One is the national anthem. As we finished the last stanza, a woman tells us what the anthem means to her.

"I am not from America," she says. "You have no idea what freedom means to others in the world. America is the land of the free, and I feel privileged to be part of what is happening here today. We have opportunities, choices, and struggles at home as well, but here you can choose the struggles you embrace. While it is true some of us come from different backgrounds, here we can attain our goals regardless of our race. I have a better chance of succeeding here than do others in different parts of the world."

Every single person on that bus had known the pain of being on the short end of experience. Each had been denied something or been excluded from places open to others.

That night I learned some very important lessons. The other torch runners and I represented what it means to help bring this world into harmony. As individuals, we were just runners. Together, however, we shared and passed the Olympic flame across the country. Collectively, we were everything.

I also learned that our time is short, but God is eternal. Twenty-eight years had passed between the time I prayed to meet Mel Counts and the night my prayer was answered.

Our Lord answers prayer in one of three ways:

Yes, you may have what you have requested.

No, I have other plans.

Not yet.

Though I had forgotten my prayer of 1968, the answer came twenty-eight years later on a bus in Salem.

How did I come to be on that bus? Each torch bearer had been nominated based on service, and the others had put far more time into their respective organizations than had I. As chair of the board of the Oregon Commission for the Blind, I contributed four to six hours every three months.

Then I realize that quite possibly I had been nominated to carry the Olympic torch because of who I am as a person, not how much time I did or did not devote to service. The Lord teaches us patience. Though I believe I have little of it, I can behave consistently toward a given task or project over a long period of time. And I have been consistently dedicated to helping people develop to their fullest potential.

On the other hand, I am weak. Paul, in the Book of Acts, teaches us about weakness and humility. Throughout much of my life, I have tried to run from blindness. I have blamed the bad things that have happened in my life to blindness. If I were sighted, I have reasoned, I could be more independent, make more money, drive fast cars, and be free. Blindness made me feel isolated from the rest of the world.

I want to share a message about what it means to surrender to others and about my struggle to allow others to help me. It is through learning how to receive from others that I have been able to understand what it means to be a servant.

Most of us do not know how to receive from God. Therefore, we do not know how to receive from others. We mask how we feel about ourselves by being busy and by striving always to be number one in our jobs and communities. Human beings are fragile and weak. And yet, it is through weakness that a person gains opportunity.

While sitting on the bus, I came to the realization that I

was ready to write my book. I had changed my perspective on what is important in life.

In the beginning, I sought power, fame, and fortune. Meeting Mel Counts taught me the importance of being human. Like me, he wanted to become successful. In fact, most people want to become successful. We have that in common, though we are also different. Acknowledging the differences, yet recognizing what we have in common, is what I have been teaching in my diversity seminars during the past decade.

Being blind, I have learned the importance of allowing others to help me with everything from getting through a cafeteria lunch line to a home improvement project.

God wants us to allow Him to help us.

God has answered many of my prayers. I have learned that prayer requests may not always be answered right away, however, because God wants us to become prepared to do his work. I am still preparing.

Looking back to that night when I carried the Olympic torch, I learned three important lessons:

1. Many things we desire in life take time. Our goals are often met or realized in very strange ways.

2. The flame of hope and peace is still alive. On that night I experienced a peace that I had never known before.

3. It is important to enjoy the journey to your destination or you may miss what life has to offer.

The formation of Hanamura Consulting showed that I, Steve Hanamura, a blind man, could make it in the world as a business owner. Yet, in achieving success, I also learned the importance of serving others. I have gained by surrendering to the process without resigning from life. The journey has had more to do with how others helped me to get here than about my own strength.

CHAPTER 2

Getting There

WHERE IS "THERE?" I BELIEVE IT IS THE destination for which we strive. When I was attending the California School for the Blind, my goals were to meet sighted people, to graduate, to go to college, to marry, and to have two sons. Goals can change. Later in my life, "there" meant striving to become a business leader.

In this culture, so much emphasis is placed on individual performance and the need to improve. During my years at the School for the Blind, I spent a lot of time wishing I could be better than I was. I wanted not only to improve, however. I wanted to be independent as well. Somehow, I felt I was not good enough unless I did achieved it for myself.

For instance, I am a runner, but I cannot run alone. I need to run with others. Prior to moving to Portland in 1980, I ran off and on with friends. But in Portland I couldn't find a running partner I could depend on. I became angry that I couldn't run when I wanted to.

One day a phone call came into the Oregon Commission for the Blind from a student, Kit Sundling-Hunt, who was working on a paper for a graduate class in special education. She needed to conduct research and write a paper on mainstreaming people with disabilities into physical education classes. For her research, she wanted to run with someone who was blind. Her advisor agreed, the Commission gave her my name, she called, and we've been running ever since. Together, we have run three marathons and more than a thousand miles of relays.

At the beginning of our running relationship, I asked myself, "Why does Kit continue to run with me when I'm so much slower?" I apologized over and over for my slowness until one day I realized that if she didn't want to run with me, she wouldn't. It was her choice. I'm glad she made it, for I would never have been able to run marathons, carry the Olympic torch, nor run the Hood to Coast Relay without a sighted person as a running partner.

As I began to examine how I was feeling about receiving help for something I wanted to do, I also considered the dynamics of our working together. It seemed to me that some of these same dynamics are in play when teams function well in the workplace.

Any team that works well is always striking a balance between the individual's success and the team's success. Though independence is important to me, blindness has allowed me to depend on others for help. I have learned how to accept help when I run, read bus signs, or read menus. Even so, I still wanted to "be my own man," so I started my own business. Later, when I learned to allow others to help me in other aspects of my life, I also learned to value the positive characteristics of life.

Running with Kit taught me about the components of successful relationships. They are commitment, accountability, empowerment, common purpose, inclusion, and trust.

1.Commitment

Commitment comes from a stance that we take. It means we do something because it is very important to us. It means we perform at the highest level of our capabilities.

Kit and I have made the commitment to one another to run together once a week. During the early years, we ran three times a week. As we both grew in our work and marriages, however, we had to restrict our running to once a week. Since Kit is faster than I, it became important that I work out on my own so that when we did meet, I would be able to do my part.

There have been many days when I didn't want to get up and run, but I knew that if I did, I'd feel better about myself both physically and emotionally. That made it worth the effort.

2. Accountability

Being accountable means we follow through with what we say we're going to do. Keeping the commitment to run made me accountable, both to myself and to Kit.

I like to close my seminars by asking each participant to write down one action step they will take as a result of being in a session with me. This pushes the envelope on accountability because we are too easily distracted from doing what we say we want to do.

For instance, I no longer make New Year's resolutions because I know I never keep them. Likewise, many organizations pass resolutions that become meaningless without an action plan or a commitment to follow through.

3. Empowerment

To be empowered means that within my capabilities I go beyond what I thought possible. For example, I never hoped to run a marathon. Yet, thanks to people like Kit, I have been empowered.

Becoming empowered means I listen to the instructions of my leader. It means I am expected to do what I say I will do. It means I make a commitment. The result is that I can feel good about myself and I take part in an event that otherwise would not have been possible for me.

There is a difference between doing something for others and enabling them to do it for themselves. Leaders of families, communities, and work groups help individuals overcome obstacles. They provide assistance by means of timely support, direction, and coaching.

It is important to emphasize that Kit was not doing something FOR me. Empowerment of others is not charity work.

Empowerment means assisting someone to better themselves, their team, or, perhaps, their family.

4. Timely Communication

Communication is the exchange of information. It is essential to our existence. The method and timeliness of the exchange affect the outcome. It is important to give and receive information in a timely manner.

On the running course, for instance, Kit and I have verbal and nonverbal methods of communication. The nonverbal method makes use of a bungee cord. Kit looks ahead and gives me information in a timely manner. I know when she tugs right, that I need instantly to move to the right. When she lifts the bungee, I know to step up or lift my foot. If she pulls back, I know to go single file.

When she communicates verbally, "step up" means move to the right and "let's go single" means we're in traffic.

Kit gives directions at exactly the moment I must act. The faster you run, the faster you must make a split-second decision to respond. Imagine making that kind of response in a personal relationship or in a team environment.

5. Common Focus

If a common focus can be agreed on, there is less possibility that individual ego needs will complicate a group effort.

Every Saturday I run ten miles with Kit. We have agreed that our pace is one mile each ten minutes. When we are finished, she drops me off at my house, then runs fifteen to twenty more miles alone at her own pace, which is one mile each seven minutes. We have agreed to run at a slower pace together than she does alone. We have agreed on the agenda or the common focus.

Employees and management who take part in team projects often have different agendas. Many times these agendas are hidden or unspoken. Unspoken agendas may explain how and why teams are not successful.

In the Hood to Coast Relay twelve runners take turns running between Mt. Hood and the beach. Each runner's ability is different; each is suited for a certain portion of the race.

Our team capitalizes on individual differences, responds to the needs of individual people, and creates an understanding of what is expected from each person regarding team objectives. We each contribute about the same financially and attend team meals together.

As a team, we have the common goal of finishing the race. We all participate in setting criteria for the team. My company is one of the sponsors of the race. Team members understand that I participate in the successful working of our team, though I am the slowest runner on the team. We have some good runners on our team, but none aspires to BE the best. We do, however, aspire, to DO our best.

6. Inclusion

People want not only to be included, but also to feel as though they have value. Recognition of individuals, however, seems to erode the success of teams.

Were it not for Kit, Randy, and others who run with me, I would not have the privilege of participating in the same events that draw sighted runners. The relationship works because Kit and Randy meet me on my level, and I feel valued for my participation.

My perspective in the beginning was that I had no value, no contribution to make. I couldn't seem to allow Kit simply to lead me. When you allow someone to lead you, I reasoned, you have a one-way caregiver relationship. I believed I was receiving care because I was deficient. I didn't realize that I had something to offer until I gave Kit and her husband, Eric, and my sons, Neil and Erik, Frequent Flyer tickets to Hawaii, where Kit and I were to run in a marathon. Still, such a gift alone is not enough to keep two parties together. It takes all the other attributes we have been discussing as well. It takes commitment, common purpose, empowerment and accountability to complete the relationship.

I am only now learning how to apply these learnings to other areas of my life.

I had believed that by starting my own business, I was a leader. And yet, I had relied on the help of others, as I had in my running. Many of them had a much broader view of my business challenges than I.

I am talking about our image of self-worth. Mine has been low at times, but I'm beginning to understand that it is when I feel the most down that I make myself available to God.

In my running at the beginning, I had been focusing only

on myself: what I was getting out of running and the fact that I couldn't take part in the events of the outside world. Kit got to me by focusing on our common purpose, which was running.

When there is reciprocity in the relationship, each person contributes, though not necessarily in the same way. I had been hung up on the need to be equal in the relationship.

In a team relationship, we need to surrender to direction by the leader. There can't be equality in the relationship, but there can be reciprocity, which holds things in place while we engage in having a relationship. I'm suggesting reciprocity can be comprised of instructions and the willingness to submit and follow.

In a reciprocal relationship, each person gives. A leader's job is to open the door for those who have not had opportunities to participate. That is what Kit, Randy and others have done for me by having me run with them. They do more for me in some situations to make it possible.

The purpose of Equal Employment Opportunity legislation was to make sure there would be no more discrimination in the workplace against people who were qualified to work, that those who were qualified would be included.

Perhaps the greatest discrepancy in the workplace is caused by the need that each of us has to feel valued. You can measure objective data, like how much you make annually, what status or position you hold, and who is the authority figure. By default, anyone who has less authority, makes lower wages, or has lower status is viewed as having less value.

But how do you place value on that which you cannot measure?

I have worked with two high tech firms that devised rating systems to determine the level of performance of each team member. In these systems, each member was ranked from top to bottom, regardless of the individual's intelligence or talent. This set up a competitive atmosphere, because one person's value was weighed against another's. This type of comparison is not conducive to reciprocal relationships.

Baseball, football, or basketball take a team effort to win, though everyone knows that star players get most of the glory or press coverage. However, there will be one or two games where a relatively unknown player helps the team get over the top to reach the championship. In this scenario, it is truly the contribution of each member that is important. I've known of many teams that had great individual players but the team as a whole could not win. Its individuals did not function as members of the team. The importance of relationships to team success is increasing, particularly with the globalization of business.

Though there are differences in expectations, talents, and expertise, there must be a point of common focus. There must also be solid understanding that reciprocity surrounds this common ground. This reciprocity is at work in a peer-to-peer relationship, a subordinate-to-boss relationship, and in a work group relationship.

7. Trust

Trust means we have confident belief in something or someone.

When I run with Kit or Randy, I trust them. Were I to trip and fall, I would not lose that trust, for I know that my welfare is of concern to them. I can trust them for direction, information, commitment, and a belief in me as a person. They work with me to help me be my best. Unfortunately, many cannot trust that their welfare is of concern in a family or in the workplace.

When we are unable to trust others, we fear loss of control over our destiny. Rating systems set up competitiveness among employees, making it virtually impossible for them to trust the employer.

Trust requires surrender. I have found that most people who are truly successful allow themselves to surrender to something or someone.

As a blind person, I thought I was doing pretty well at surrendering. After all, I asked people for help every day. I asked them to read the number on the bus, read documents to me, or help me find the right concourse in the airport.

Though I've had to depend on others, I've also felt the need to become as independent as possible. How could I do both?

In reality, I had not been surrendering. I wouldn't let others help me where I really needed help — in my spirit. In fact, I was and am still too proud to allow others to help me where I truly have needed help.

Perhaps surrendering to someone else's authority or to a process is the sign of a true human being. In the Bible, men are instructed to submit themselves to Christ and the church. Women are instructed by the Bible to submit themselves to their husbands.

I believe that Kit has become a better runner since she allowed herself to surrender to her coaches' instructions. If her coach directs her to run ten miles on Monday and thirty miles on Saturday, she does. If the coach says, "Take Friday off," she takes Friday off. Some authority figures have been known to abuse their subordinates, thereby compounding the challenges to surrendering to another's learnings. I know this for a fact. When I am out on the running course, I do exactly as I'm told. When an airplane pilot listens to air traffic control, he or she does exactly as told.

We resist surrendering because most of us think we will not be able to exert our individuality in a given situation. To the contrary, I find that in surrendering, I discover even more of myself.

The term surrender has been confused with resignation. Resignation means you give up, you stop doing. Issues of trust and safety make it hard for us to surrender.

This is what is so beautiful about being in God's kingdom. As I strive to build my relationship with God, I know that I can surrender all my challenges to Him. Being human, however, I sometimes do not wait for His directives.

I have difficulty surrendering to God or to a leader, coach, or boss because I am proud. I like to be recognized for my accomplishments.

It is important to be able to celebrate an accomplishment but at the same time to remember that at no one time did we achieve that accomplishment alone. Somewhere or sometime someone has helped us acquire the skills necessary to become successful. Individual effort is still required, however. God allows us to choose whether we wish to follow His directive.

I know that I must surrender two things.

First, I surrender to myself by accepting my strengths and limitations. I know I will not become a major league sports announcer, though I've long wanted to be, but I know that I can make other contributions.

Secondly, I surrender to my Lord. I know He has given me gifts for doing certain things on earth. I choose the level or degree of involvement based on the talents or gifts I have been given.

Most employees who are dissatisfied on the job are no longer involved or engaged. They have become resigned. They are biding their time until retirement or are hoping they will win the lottery.

Many corporate executives have asked me, "How can we get our employees to partner with us to accomplish our objectives?" A partnership is fifty-fifty, whereas, in a reciprocal relationship, both parties are independent. Interdependence draws on different levels of skill and talent. In God's kingdom, we partner with Him to accomplish His purpose. Although I am concentrating on accomplishing something, I know that He is the commander. For a workplace partnership to succeed, employers must create an authentic atmosphere of acceptance and trust. The employee must respect authority and be able to see the benefit of experience.

In all aspects of my life I am now learning the importance of allowing others to help me. If business falls off, my wife, Becky, takes a job to help us meet our financial obligations. I could not run our household without her help. Nor could our business survive without the talent and know-how of the computer people who help me. The key to success is learning how to create an atmosphere where we can allow others to help us instead of trying to do everything ourselves.

I'm learning that with the help of others I can become involved in things that wouldn't have been possible otherwise. I use discernment in selecting people who can serve as mentors or authority figures to me. If we are now autonomous and would like to begin allowing others to help us, there are some things we can do to get started:

1. Identify people we'd like to model ourselves after.

2. Examine how they got to where they are today. What kind of help did they need?

3. What are their talents, skills, and resources?

4. Where did they find resources to increase their ability to become successful?

5. What kind of discipline did it take for them to get there?

We need to ask ourselves how long we think their success will last. For many, success is short-lived. Now we are ready to look at what it means to have eternal success.

Being successful is not as important as being significant. Successful people come and go. My friend John Griffiths says that after age forty it's time to look at what it means to have significance instead of what it means to be successful. If we can let go of our pride and replace it with a willingness to let others serve us, we will be taking the first step to understanding how God is serving us through the talents and gifts of others.

CHAPTER 3

About Love

I AM FIVE YEARS OLD, PREPARING TO BOARD a train with twenty-nine other blind children. Tears are streaming down my cheeks. "Why do I have to go away?" I cry.

"Because we love you," reply Mom and Dad.

The train is bound from Los Angeles to the San Francisco Bay Area. We children are headed for Berkeley, to the California School for the Blind, the only school of its kind in California where blind children can obtain an education. Until that moment in the train station, I had been excited about going to school. But I realize suddenly that my parents are going to return home, while I must remain at school.

Not until many years later did I understand it had been painful for my parents to let go of me. That moment in the train station, however, and for years afterward, I was so absorbed in my own misery that I could not see theirs. Their decision hurt, but they had a vision in which their son would become successful in life. That success would require an education.

Now I know that when you are committed to the people you love, you do what it takes to help them become successful. In our case it meant we had to be separated during my formative years so that I could make it later in life.

During the writing of this chapter, I am fifty-two years old and have my own business. I guess their vision paid off.

During those early years, however, I could not see where their vision would lead me. Instead, I felt imprisoned. For days, I stood at the window of the school, facing south, wishing I could be home. As the weeks and months passed, Mom sent postcards daily. I saved each in a shoebox for many years. I could not yet understand what I know now: that the real prison we live in is constructed within us, not outside.

My memories of being at the blind school those first few years are still a blur. All I knew was that I was someplace I didn't want to be.

When I was nine, I was inspired by Danny Lambert, a classmate who was much older than I and also very religious. He conducted weekly Bible studies at the school. Since my church had given me a Braille Bible a year earlier, I thought, "Why not take part?" Suddenly, I became excited. I don't remember that I understood much in the Bible at that age. What I do remember was how powerful Jesus was, especially when he healed a blind man.

I hoped to be healed in such a way, for then I could go home to live with my family. I could be "normal."

Every night for two years I prayed that God would heal my eyesight. But there was no response to my prayer. I was miserable. The worst part was having to say good-bye every Christmas and fall to Mom, Dad, and my brother, Mike.

The only thing that made me feel better was my physical education class, where I was on a tumbling team. We performed at half-time during basketball games around the San Francisco Bay Area. Because of that, I became increasingly involved in sports.

I developed a love of baseball. I listened faithfully to recreated radio broadcasts of major league ball games featuring the Brooklyn Dodgers and the Philadelphia Phillies.

And I became emotionally involved in this great sport. Not understanding at that time that the home team always goes to bat last, I grew to hate the Dodgers when they had home field advantage. Later, I became a diehard Dodgers fan when the team moved to Los Angeles.

Our physical education teacher and his wife, Dr. and Mrs. Buell, were deeply committed to helping blind children develop their interest in physical education. They dedicated themselves to involving us in physical education and scouting activities on weekends.

We played with a softball the size of a big grapefruit. Dr. Buell was pitcher and also told each batter when to swing. Can you imagine what it's like to be blind, to swing a bat when you are told to swing, and then to connect solidly with the ball? The exhilaration is incredible.

There were rules for our play. If we hit the ball, we ran to first. If the ball was caught in the air or before it stopped rolling, it was counted as a fly ball.

If you can imagine being blind and playing baseball, maybe you can imagine what it took to go hiking or to be on a tumbling team. Taking part in these sports gave me welcome relief from the otherwise miserable feelings I was experiencing about being blind and away from home.

Just the other night, while I was preparing to write this chapter, I noticed a special television program on past NBA greats like Bill Russell, who led the Boston Celtics to eleven national championships.

I couldn't believe it! I'm writing a book, and Bill Russell shows up again in my life. He had been important in my past when I was on tumbling teams that performed at half-time during many of his college games.

Despite my misery and prayers, God hadn't yet given me my eyesight by the time I turned thirteen. So there I was, dwelling on blindness. I was mad. The world clearly wasn't fair.

Various people react differently to childhood pain. I have seen some try to bury the past, while others have dwelt on the past as an excuse for not being able to perform.

And yet some good things come from pain. I had a sudden realization that this experience had been very good for me at a time when I'd cut off feelings in order not to remember. When you cut off your feelings, you also cut off joy.

I believe we are called upon to understand in what ways

our past has implications for the way we make choices or treat others. To bury our past and to look forward oblivious of how it has had an impact on us is wrong. Yet, dwelling on the past exclusively is not good either.

One August, on summer break from school, I sat in our breezeway at home asking God these questions: "Why me, Lord? Why am I blind? Why can't I read the sports page? Why can't I play baseball. Why can't I be a normal kid?"

It didn't occur to me at the time to ask, "Why NOT me?"

That summer, when no one was at home, I would sit in the breezeway and throw my shoes at the other wall, retrieve them, throw them back, again and again, thinking. Finally, as I prepared to return to school, I said to myself, "This is too painful. The Bible study doesn't work. I prayed to God. He didn't heal me. I have no control over whether or not I go to school or stay home."

And so I made a conscious decision to shut down my feelings. I was going to find a way to avoid feeling the pain. If kids made fun of me, I wouldn't cry. I developed a strategy for becoming like my television heroes, Matt Dillon, U.S. Marshall, and Cheyenne Bodie, frontier scout. Both were big, tough, and quiet. They got the job done and said little about how they felt. During this same summer, my voice was changing. I knew I could sound tough, strong, and larger than I really was, as long as I did most of my interactions by phone.

In September, I went to school three days late because Mom and Dad agreed to let me go to the Los Angeles County

Fair in Pomona for the first time. When I finally made it to school, I had to take a science test, which Mr. Huckins had postponed for me. I received a D.

Despite that low grade, eighth grade seemed off to a good start. My plan not to feel anything seemed to be working. I put myself out there and became the first eighth grader to become student body president.

In time, I became fairly successful by world standards. I graduated from high school and college, married, and held jobs in education, government, and the corporate world. In 1986 I opened my own business. It was in graduate school, where my major was counseling, that I began to allow others into my world while also keeping myself protected. When pain is too difficult to handle, we learn how to mask our feelings so well that we may not even know what we feel. There have been times when I have shared my feelings, but have been told that, in fact, I wasn't feeling.

When there is pain, we do one of two things.

We either do whatever it takes to hide the pain so we can function, or we allow the pain to bleed all over everyone else. I thought that I was unique because I was tough, shy, and quiet. However, there are many of us, both men and women, who do that.

It is not that I hate love. It is the impact of what happens when love hurts that I hate. Maybe what I really hate are pain and conflict.

Here are two questions for us to explore: How do lessons from early in our lives impact the way we live our lives today? What are the implications of the choices we make in future encounters with people? Perhaps something happened in our youth where we consciously or unconsciously said, "I am never going to feel that pain again," or "I won't let that happen to me again."

I am intrigued when someone says, during an argument, "I don't care" or "Fine, have it your way." What is really being said is "things are not fine, but I am withdrawing from the conflict." By withdrawing, I can still feel successful. I may not even know that I am in pain.

What I have come to learn is that the pain stays with us but gets redirected somewhere else in our bodies. I tend to feel pain or tension in my shoulders, stomach, or lower back. These parts of my body let me know when something is not right.

Approximately one year before the writing of this book I was doing some work with a city's police department. One policeman's question was about an apparent lack of conscience in youth today when they shoot people and seem to feel no remorse. Do they feel no love for others?

While preparing a speech for a health care organization, I was approached by the person who hired me just minutes before I was to give the speech. "Steve," he said, "You need to modify your speech."

"Really?" I said. "How?"

"We want you to include your thoughts about the O.J.Simpson trial," he said.

"The O.J. trail?" I asked, "What for?"

"There is a tremendous gap between how white employees and African American employees feel about the verdict," he replied. "These differences in viewpoint are fracturing our workplace."

"Okay," I replied.

Actually what the O.J. Simpson trial did was to surface differences that already existed. We were finally saying color makes a difference. We no longer were hiding the issue under the table by saying, "I don't see color, I just see people."

As I worked through my thoughts about the O.J. Simpson trial, I told the employees to close their eyes and to raise their hands if they thought O.J.Simpson was guilty. Next, I asked them to raise their hands if they thought O.J.Simpson was innocent. Finally, I told them that what they thought didn't matter. I said that what mattered was our inability to sit in the same room and have a conversation about our different viewpoints. I said, "We are unable to talk about how our past experiences have influenced the way we see or experience the world today."

The real issues that the O.J. Simpson trial surfaced were about domestic violence. In my rides with the police department, I noted that two out of three phone calls from the dispatcher's office were about domestic violence. It has been estimated that ninety percent of all crimes committed today are perpetrated by people who know the victim.

Even families members who love one another have problems. The family unit is breaking up. Respect and love have gone down the tubes.

What is love? Is it passion and romance? While there is a place for both, love has more breadth and depth. True love comes from the heart of one person and is transferred to another.

There are at least three types of love:

philia: brotherly/sisterly/friendly love

eros: erotic love

agape: God's love

It is God's love that is missing from families, our homes, and places of work. Even in Christian homes, we have not yet mastered the art of loving. While I am not an expert on love, I do know that it is something that most of us want but don't know how to get.

My work with the police was disturbing because they deal with people who appear to have no conscience, but who in reality have lost their ability to love and respect, who think nothing of destroying property and lives, who have become numb to awareness or responsibility for anyone but themselves.

I would like to boldly say that we can and should be creating a sense of love in the workplace. I am not an expert on the subject of love, nor am I a theologian who can espouse church doctrine. What I do know is that my relationship with Jesus Christ has offered me the opportunity to revisit my initial feelings about being stoic and not expressing my feelings. I know how we are suffering from an inability to be in effective relationships.

When you love, you make yourself vulnerable. The ability or inability to love also affects the way we hope or dream for the future. Do you dream expectantly (meaning you expect to have your dreams realized)? Or do you dream hopefully (meaning that you hope someday your dream will be realized)?

If you dream hopefully, you usually have a disclaimer, like "It would be nice but I don't know if it will really happen" or "I hope for something good to happen in this situation, but I'm not going to hope for it too much in case it doesn't happen, for then I won't feel hurt."

When pain becomes too great, we decide not to expect the best. We hope just to "get by." That's what my dad said he wanted after he came out of a World War II internment camp. He borrowed $1,500 to start a service station with which he could support his family. He hoped the station would do well. It was in a good location next to a freeway exit. He figured that customers would need to get gas as they left the freeway. Later, he told me that the business never reached its full potential.

In truth, he had wanted more than just to "get by." He had also wanted to provide for me and my brother Mike. He and Mom were trying to do this at a time when Japanese-Americans were not being treated fairly. Both Mom and Dad are incredible people. Mike and I have learned so much from their example of how to live through pain and yet not let pain stop you from going where you want to go.

Mom and Dad did what it took just to get by, and their getting by made it possible for my brother and me to be successful. Sometimes you need simply to be rigorous. There are times when you have to be with the pain. And there are times when you mask your feelings. Sometimes you simply endure.

Remember always to be open to change.

When pain becomes unbearable, we lower our expectations. Sometimes we mask feelings of hurt. When we close off feelings, when we stop hoping for the best, we run the risk of shutting out potential opportunities. We need to remain open both to the hurt and what we can learn from it.

The source of pain may be communication differences at home or on the job. Communication differences may be related to style, personality makeup, individual experience, ethnic influence, or racial differences. Until we learn how to agree to disagree with each other and to do so effectively, individuals will fear their integrity is not intact.

If we lose hope, trust, and belief that things can change, we will continue to either shut down or shut off.

I suggest that there are four stages we go through when dealing with pain or conflict.

1. Numbing

During this phase we make a decision consciously or unconsciously not to feel pain. This behavior can be influenced by our culture. In some cultures there are mores about how we are to behave relative to pain. The Japanese culture teaches us not to complain. In order not to complain about conflict or pain, the Japanese either avoid it, turn to drink, or commit suicide. These models eventually lead us to numb ourselves from the pain in order to function.

Numbing ourselves against pain is not a strategy that leads to success, though I shut off feelings and did quite well (or so I thought) at the age of thirteen. However, when you numb yourself to pain, you miss other possibilities. In 1988 I met Karen Carnahan and Marsia Gunter, both of whom are business coaches. They told me that I was too independent. I would not allow others to help me.

"What do you mean I'm too independent?" I asked. "I ask people to help me everyday." (*"What's the menu in the restaurant?" "What's the number of that bus?"*)

They explained that I did not allow myself to be helped with ideas, thoughts, and feelings about who I am as a person. When we numb ourselves, we do not see what is possible in terms of hopes, dreams, and reality.

I do not want to discount people who must function in survival mode. We all do at times. During those times, we do not dwell on negative feelings but numb ourselves to pain or hurt so we can function in the world. Short-term numbing is okay as long as it doesn't become our only mechanism for solving our problems.

2. Thumbing

There are three types of people: There are do-ers, be-ers,

and victims. The do-ers get things done. They function well in crisis conditions, many times blocking out their own feelings and those of other people. They are detail oriented. You can count on them.

Be-ers are people who wear their emotions on their sleeves. They are expressive of their thoughts, feelings, and actions. You never have to worry about hidden agendas with be-ers. They are very relationship oriented.

Victims see the world as an awful place where anything that happens to them is someone else's fault. Thumbing takes its shape in victims. Whatever goes wrong is not their fault. They say things like, "Management did this to me, and there is nothing I can do about it."

I do not mean to discount acts of violence or other tragedies in which people are truly victimized or violated. The key is how we choose to react. Victims thumb a ride like hitchhikers who ride in someone else's car to reach their destination. Victims do this because they have difficulty seeing other options.

Another form of thumbing occurs when we keep ourselves busy in order to overcompensate for what is missing in our lives.

3. Drumming

During the summer of my eighth grade year I joined a band. I was one of three drummers. One played snare, the other played percussion, and I played bass.

I began to dream about becoming as good as my favorite

jazz drummer, Cozy Cole. During one practice session, a drummer was absent. That meant I was to play both bass and snare. The snare drummer had a very important part. I had been listening to it and knew how it should sound. The moment of truth came. It was time for me to play.

I bombed terribly.

The director gave me several chances to get it right, but I just couldn't do it. The good news, however, was that I played really well on the bass drum. I was steady, consistent, and on beat. I could be counted on to keep the band on beat.

The drumming phase of life is when we become consistent. We live in the middle with our routine.

On the surface, it can look good. For instance, I knew two families who appeared to have solid, stable, consistent lives, but who eventually split up.

When we drum, we are consistent, predictable, and have a routine. What may be missing, though, is the ability to move outside our comfort zone.

This may mean taking the risk of telling someone that things are not well, for instance, or that we want change. If these needs are not addressed, the conflict goes underground. The fabric of a relationship may begin to tear apart.

Although drumming can help us avoid major conflict, it may also keep us from experiencing a level of love that can be much more invigorating. If we want our love to be fuller, we must take risks. When we risk, we upset routine and predictability.

As I get older, I am beginning to realize that nothing

remains the same, nothing except God's consistency.

It is hard to find balance between routine and risk. If our need for safety overrides everything else, we may avoid taking risks to keep from getting hurt. If we do not risk, we may also lose spontaneity. Drumming along in life needs a mix of spontaneity and routine, a balance of both head and heart. The fear of pain or loss is the real robber here, because it keeps us from experiencing life to its fullest.

4. Humming

Humming embodies the consistency of drumming and the ability to find inner peace with self and God. When we surrender our life to Him, new possibilities open up to us.

During the humming phase, a person understands the ups and downs of life, the highs and lows of what it means to love others.

My parents had the strength and courage to send me to the School for the Blind. They made that decision from a "head position," not from their emotions. Acting on their emotions only would have kept me at home.

As this is being written, I have just said good-bye to them, as we put them on a plane for home after four marvelous days that culminated with Neil's graduation. Shortly after they left, I felt panic and sadness, the kind I felt when I was seven or eight or thirteen. What will happen if I don't see them again? I hadn't told them how much they mean to me.

Now I know that I can allow these feelings to be there, instead of blocking them. If I were to block them, I would have missed the joy of being together. Maturity does not help painful feelings go away. You have to learn how to be with the painful feelings and push through to something fuller and deeper. I once wished we could live in a conflict-free society. I still wish that, but know that this dream is not possible.

I must live with all types of feelings. I am learning how not to hate love. It's still frightening at times, but I can say it's worth the risk. Risk equals pain, uncertainty, joy, and peace. The final outcome of that is that you can learn to be with love.

Let's resurrect it for our world. In the humming phase, we experience moments of true peace.

For me, that moment came on May 6, 1996, while I was carrying the Olympic Torch. I knew then that there would be times when I would experience conflict and discomfort, but I also learned that there would be other times when I would be in alignment with the power of the Holy Spirit and that even in the midst of trials, I could be at peace.

Sports teams talk about how momentum or flow can change the course of a game. When we are humming, we take full advantage of momentum to do our best work.

CHAPTER 4

Creating a Positive Self-Image

HE'S LATE. MY TOWN CAR DRIVER, WAYNE, agreed last night to pick me up at 6:45 this morning. I am to be in Gresham by 7:30 for my seminar. It is nearly seven now. There's heavy traffic this time of the morning.

I call Wayne on his cell phone.

"Hello?"

"Where are you?" I try to sound pleasant.

"I'm at Allen and Murray," he says. "I'll be there in ten minutes."

"Okay," I reply. We hang up. Fifteen minutes later he still hasn't arrived. I call again. "Now where are you?" I ask.

"I'm pulling into your driveway," he replies.

As I get into the car, Wayne explains he had a customer pickup at 5 a.m. for the airport. After he finished with that fare, he planned to come to my house, but his boss, Aaron, had promised another client that Wayne would pick him up.

"But I'll be late to get Steve," Wayne protested. "Don't worry," his boss said. "You'll make it."

Wayne was caught in a bind. He wanted to obey his boss and yet he wanted to be on time for his other customers. So he tried to work in the extra fare. As a result, he was late getting to me.

I am now presented with an opportunity for responding to Wayne. Since he is a good friend, I screen what I will say. Then I realize that even if he were not a friend, I should still screen what I say.

"Wayne, I need to have a business conversation with you which is different from a friendship talk," I begin. "Being late does not work for me. Perhaps you can convey to Aaron that if it happens again, I can no no longer utilize your services."

Wayne is in between jobs and can ill afford to disobey Aaron. And yet because of our friendship, Wayne is striving to make things right.

He tells me he will give me two free fares as compensation for my inconvenience. He also makes a commitment to convey to Aaron my displeasure. Though Wayne wants to preserve his job, he is willing to risk speaking up to maintain his own integrity.

I accept his offer. A few days later I learn that Aaron did

not respond favorably. He did not say, "I'm sorry, we'll have to rethink that next time." Instead, he said he had to make money, that fares could be worked in. There was no apology.

What is the message in this experience?

In some seminars, I ask participants to identify the three major diseases in the world. They come up with answers like cancer, AIDS, and heart failure. I acknowledge their ideas, then pose the possibility that the diseases that truly plague us today are the need to be number one, guilt, and depression.

1. Being Number One

This disease grows out of the attitude that everything is done "my way." In other words, being number one supersedes how we treat people. It is this attitude that was driving Wayne's boss when he ordered him to pick up another fare at the expense of being late for me. Aaron wanted to make more money. Greed and profit drive most people's behavior to be number one.

While on a business trip in California, I stayed at a hotel that served a buffet breakfast. A member of the staff of the hotel guest services offered to go through the line and bring breakfast to my room.

When I came back to the hotel for a second stay, he asked, with no prompting, "What would you like for breakfast tomorrow morning?" The third time the offer was still in place. I wrote a letter to the manager to acknowledge this individual.

"I am so grateful for that letter you wrote," the person from guest services told me the fourth time I came back. "No one has ever done that before. You made my day."

I mused over how I had made his day and realized that he makes my day every time I go there. To me, this is what we must see as the image of ourselves as workers no matter what position or status we hold. Staying in nice hotels, being executives of major corporations, or being holders of Frequent Flyer cards are not necessarily what make us number one.

2. Feeling Guilty

Guilt can paralyze us. A person of courage can turn into a person of fear and guilt if someone else's standards are not met. We fear what others may think about us. We become so tied up inside we cannot be ourselves.

People who have more than others may become defensive for what they have. Does this mean people who have more must forfeit profit or lower their standards? Not at all. When we strive to work from Christ's image, our position in a corporation, school, government agency, community, or economic level doesn't matter. We can all be number one in the way we relate to others.

3. Depression

Depression is the most subtle of the three workplace diseases. It shows up when workers shut down, withdraw, and leave the workplace itself. I am convinced that we must not separate our workplace image from that of Christ's image.

The dialogue in which Wayne and I were engaged is an example of how to treat one another in Christ's image. In contrast, another limo driver who was late picking up a fare was punched to the ground and stomped on by his frustrated and angry customer.

I must confess that my behavior with Wayne was influenced by our friendship and the fact that we attend the same church. Being Wayne's friend held me accountable. I sought to understand. Shouldn't we be doing that in all our interactions with people?

Depression has infiltrated our workplace because those in authority have not done a good job of setting a climate in which people can flourish.

I am not talking about other forces within an individual that may be causing depression, nor am I trying to offer clinical reasons for depression. I am referring to the part we play in influencing how the world can be for others. I am talking about speaking encouraging words, instead of words that put people down.

I will never be the best because there is always someone better ahead of me or waiting to take my place. What I can strive for, however, is to operate at my best.

We walk the line between striving for success and feeling too pumped up about ourselves. I want to make sure that we are clear that it is okay to strive to be good at what we do. What we must remember is not to take ourselves too seriously. Our accomplishments will be forgotten or considered irrelevant in a short time.

Perhaps it is helpful to explore some pitfalls for developing and maintaining a positive self-image.

The first is envy. It is sometimes hard to distinguish between admiration and envy. When you visit someone's home it is easy to say things like, "Their family runs so smoothly. They have a lot of nice things."

At times colleagues have also envied me. I have been asked, "How did you get THAT contract?" What they were really saying was that they wished THEY had the contract. The time we spend envying someone else's possessions or qualities is better spent developing our own talents and gifts from within. We may also need to accept the fact that we don't have the same talents and gifts that got another person what they received or achieved.

When we focus on what others have, we are not available to develop or bring out the talents and gifts God has given us. Early in my career I envied what some others had, but later I learned of others who envied me. Some felt that I was receiving accolades only because I am blind and went beyond people's expectations of what a blind facilitator could do. There are times when I must be aware of compliments for that reason.

The second pitfall is trying to be someone you are not. I have seen individuals and organizations try to duplicate something that has become successful. Rarely does this work. It is true that there are skills or systems you can put into place that help you draw from the experiences of others. In each case, however, you must be able to bring out what is you.

I admire Vin Scully, the voice of the Los Angeles Dodgers and the CBS World Series broadcasts. Although I have never met him, I have tried to emulate some of his nuances.

Another person I admire is Jack Kiekel, friend and minister. He, like Scully, has a deep base voice. We have that in common. It would be ridiculous for me to try to be like either one of them. However, they both have deep, sincere feelings toward their respective audiences. They convey knowledge of their subject matter and a love for their relationships. They also make their comments relevant and understandable to the people they talk with. You feel they are talking to you personally.

Ever since I have known Jack, he has respected me for who I am. He knew me as a college student, a counselor, and a consultant. He never pulled rank because he is older. He related to me and encouraged me in response to who I am and not for who I am not.

When you see a good thing, your tendency is to duplicate. Imitate doesn't mean copy. In the attempt to imitate we may develop similar attributes in ourselves, in a situation, or in a relationship.

The third pitfall for developing a positive self-image is bragging or boasting. Sometimes it is hard to know the difference between bragging and delighting in what you did well. I have occasionally been the last to acknowledge when things went well. People have complimented me, and I have discounted the compliment by saying something like, "I was just lucky." The problem with this response is that I downplayed my talent.

In 1989 I was receiving business coaching from a group of people who were trying to get me to take responsibility for my skills and talents. They wanted me to learn how to promote myself and my business.

In the Asian culture, I was brought up not to talk about myself too much. You gave credit to others but not to yourself. What was revealed to me was that I was underground about credit. I carried myself in an arrogant manner, but wouldn't necessarily speak about it publicly.

Arrogance is a form of bragging. It means elevating ourselves to a superior position. This elevation shouldn't be confused with having confidence in who we are and what skills we have. The best and most highly revered leaders are those people who evoke a sense of humility. It doesn't mean they are spineless. To the contrary, they have demonstrated great tact, skill, and artistry in order to achieve.

A fourth pitfall is negative self-talk. We relive past experiences and revive comments from others that may cause us not to believe ourselves. The fear of failure and the fear of what others think make it virtually impossible for us to feel like we can be successful. Trust me, I've been there. When I feel down, it is impossible for me to feel good about myself.

Here are some things that have worked for me.

I set aside time daily to be in God's Word and to pray. I know that many of you may not have Jesus Christ in your life. To you I would say develop some way to get in touch with your spirituality.

My relationship with Christ serves as the centerpiece for all other aspects of my life. Before even getting out of bed each day, I pray about those things I will be doing. When I don't begin my day in prayer, I get off track.

I read the Bible daily, once from the New Testament and once from the Old Testament. On hectic days I may shorten one of my readings to five minutes. Over the long haul, it helps me deal with conflict. Without this discipline, I can lose focus. If I lose focus, I may also lose my temper.

I also work to develop my life in Christ's image. I don't parrot scripture. To be Christlike means that I allow myself to develop and be who I am. I am open to accepting differences in others.

Each person has something unique to offer. Each should be encouraged to bring those attributes to the table. To be Christlike means that in His image I can appreciate, respect, value, and embrace differences. I can also see what we have in common and can bring about harmony.

A third strategy is to hang out with people who are positive and who can serve as role models for being positive during negative times.

As a Christian, am I going to praise God when a loved one is sick or killed? Probably not. What I can do is learn how to ask for God's presence. I can ask Him to reveal to me what I am to learn from this situation. Being around positive people can give us new insights on how to overcome adversity.

We have an opportunity to put into practice this notion of dependence and surrender. If we operate from Christ's image, new possibilities open up for us. If everything seems hopeless, we can plan that things will be different by developing a visual picture of how we want our life to be. If we follow God, we may experience some redirection at times, but what we are really looking for is internal peace and not external gain. Don't give up the dream.

CHAPTER 5

Embracing Change

IT'S SATURDAY NIGHT AND I'M STANDING ON the choir risers at church, feeling dissatisfied. We have a full orchestra this evening. There are about three-hundred people worshipping. I notice the woodwind instruments sound flat. As we start to sing, I can tell the voice of someone near me is off.

Suddenly, I ask myself, "What am I doing here?"

It just doesn't feel right to be celebrating Easter Sunday on Saturday, though admittedly there are also two services tomorrow. As communion is served, I begin to realize that I am being extremely critical. After all, it doesn't matter when I worship. I pray and do my Bible study on days other than Sunday. Is there another cause of my being so critical?

Then it hits me. I'm writing a chapter on the importance

of tradition and yet here I am in church on Saturday night, participating in the breaking of tradition. After all, Easter should be celebrated on Sunday, not Saturday.

My response to this experience provides me with an opportunity to examine the meaning of tradition in a much more personal way. Easter, for me personally, not religiously, has been a time of stress, confusion, and hope. As a child I counted on seeing Mom, Dad, or Mike every Easter. Two of them would come to the School for the Blind to see me. Easter Sunday they went home and I stayed at school. Later in life, Easter became a time to gather with family.

The confusion arises this Saturday night because I know Easter is to be a day of joy, but I find myself in turmoil.

The choir experience on Easter Saturday is wake-up call. It has signaled me to appreciate tradition, but at the same time not to get so bogged down that I don't appreciate change or the people around me.

Where does tradition come from? What is its value? I think tradition provides order, structure, predictability, and credibility. Traditions gives us something to count on. They are formed in the roots of our culture.

We live in a fast-paced, multi-cultural society where it is difficult to understand what is tradition and what is not.

As an individual, I belong to several different cultures at the same time. I belong to such cultures as Japanese, blind, male, Christian, entrepreneur, and runner. Each has a set of expectations, beliefs, or stereotypes.

Historically we have thought of cultures as pertaining to

our ethnic background. And yet culture is a system or domain from which we gather our roots and form values. Each domain or system has its own set of values that determine how we behave, or how we think we should behave.

As I grow and mature, I learn that I am part of several domains, but within each domain I strive to form my own unique individual characteristics. They are shaped by my past. Life patterns or expectations may be based on how secure I feel within myself. That sense of security may derive from traditions that I have experienced. Each time we go into a new group, job, or community it is useful to learn the traditions and beliefs.

I once heard someone define the difference between men and women in this way: Boys go to school, graduate from high school, go to college, meet a woman, graduate, marry, and get a job. Girls go to school, graduate from high school, go to college, meet a man, get married, maybe graduate, and stay at home.

This scenario has set the stage for our perceptions of traditional marriage. And yet we are not robots. We were created to exercise our individual talents and gifts. How do we exercise our individuality while acknowledging our history?

Let's visit four attributes that give value to traditions.

1. Order

Order creates the framework from which I work. It helps

me make sense out of my world, particularly in times of chaos and crisis. I organize my thoughts, create the agendas, and put things in a specific order or position to get done. Order helps me practice efficiency.

2. Structure

Once the framework has been created, behaviors or action steps can be implemented. They are based on an orderly arrangement. People know where they are supposed to go and what they are supposed to do. Structure is considered to be a way of creating freedom. The boundaries are fairly clear under a given structure.

Becky and I created a structure so I can find the right clothes to wear. In our closet we have stacked clothes bins. My undershirts are in one bin, running shirts in another, and T-shirts in a third. When I want to go out, I have a structure that frees me to choose a shirt to wear.

In like manner, employees need a structure from which to work, and they may differ on the amount of structure they need to do their jobs.

Before my Easter experience in the choir, I had been so structurally rigid that I had not seen other possibilities. I had become accustomed to the order and structure that said Easter music could be sung only on Sunday and not on Saturday. That was the structure on which I had celebrated Easter over the years.

Though employees need structure, it can also limit new ways of addressing problems.

3. Predictability

Traditions have a way of creating predictability. In a world where change occurs faster than we can manage it, predictability is important. As the employment picture becomes more difficult to understand, workers find themselves in the position of not knowing where or how they will get their next paycheck. Thirty or forty years ago, a person could expect to remain with one employer for life. It was predictable. In those days we were not dealing with issues of downsizing.

4. Credibility

Tradition, if carried out over a long period of time, evokes credibility, particularly when you are talking about individual behavior. There is overlap between predictability and credibility. When I came home from the School for the Blind, I could count on my parents taking me to a certain Chinese restaurant in Los Angeles before going home to Upland. Even when my brother Mike brought a girlfriend to meet me when he was sixteen, we still went to the restaurant. Traditions are established over a period of time. Sometimes they are repetitious, but if we know that we can count on something that happened in the past, we believe we can count on it in the future as well. I asked a group of high school students to tell me about a tradition in their house. Many could not come up with one. Perhaps this is an indicator of how things have changed and serves notice to us that we are losing our traditions.

Another tradition for me is to eat hot dogs and peanuts at Dodger Stadium. There is nothing better. At the modern-day ballparks around the country, fast food services and restaurants are serving all types of food. I, however, out of deference to tradition, will order hot dogs and peanuts at Dodger Stadium every time. This is my tradition.

Traditions create a sense of expectancy, helping us establish order and make sense out of the world. They provides us with fond memories.

What happens, though, if you grew up with negative traditions? What happens if you must mix with others whose traditions are different from yours?

One downside to tradition is that we can become stuck in our ways and have difficulty adapting to change. For example, there may be some good food other than hot dogs and peanuts at the ballpark. I may have missed out on something.

A second downside: By sticking to my tradition, I may be setting up a situation in which my way is right and the other person is wrong.

Finally, tradition can create unnecessary conflict between the individual and groups of people who have different traditions

What happens if women want to work in traditionally male jobs? Are the women wrong for wanting to do that? Do new conflicts develop because of a desire to break with tradition? What can we do to prepare for change?

In the one-world construct, we are all global citizens, but

you wouldn't know that by our behavior. In the United States, English is the central language, but difficulty may arise when employees want to speak a different language in the lunchroom or by the water cooler. That, in part, is due to our tradition of English being the spoken language. It is something we know and believe. It keeps us informed and included.

What do we do now that the world's demographics are shifting? Do we declare the American way the right way?

There are two sets of dynamics that I believe are contributing to our dilemma. The first is that we are confusing tradition with issues of power, equity, and authority. Second, there is a need for us to strengthen our ability to change.

In most organizational and family structures, there is a hierarchy for how things are to be done. Each group has its own set of norms, standards, and behaviors. These standards were derived from a core set of values. The problem then becomes who has the right or authority to see that these norms and standards are enforced.

Power is usually thought of as force or leverage, which translate into authority. If someone has force or leverage over us, that status implies that we are weaker or less than they are. It is this force or leverage that in part has created the need for individuality to flourish. Traditional behavior can unintentionally stifle creativity.

Becky and I got into a heated discussion once about how often the boys could have soda pop. As our voices rose, I hollered that Sprite had been a staple at our house. Becky's reply was that at her house soda pop was a special privilege once a month.

We had differing traditions. Unknowingly, what Becky and I had been allowed as children was driving our responses to one another as adults. Similarly, what we bring from other workplaces informs how we solve problems. Our personal backgrounds influence us. Traditions can affect how we decide to solve a problem.

Issues of power and authority are difficult enough in a family when parents have differing traditions. What happens in management teams? How do members convey to employees what is expected if the managers individually come from different backgrounds?

Once we see it, we can let go of our past and live in the present. Still, we need to be aware of how our past has influenced us.

Tradition can serve as a catalyst for creating a positive environment where people can have a framework and still be in discussion related to change. In some situations it is necessary for an authority figure to have the final say in order to get things moving.

I believe that people often confuse the meaning of tradition. They misinterpret it as succumbing to authority. There is conflict, discourse, and tension when two people or two groups try to reach a goal or develop an understanding of each other's perspective.

Those of us who have had difficulty dealing with tradition may be struggling with perceptions of not feeling valued, not getting what we want, or being run over roughshod.

In today's society, there are groups of people who appear to have no respect for authority. If I am to do as told by a manager, parent, or other authority figure, I must feel equity in the relationship. Equity means that at some point my ideas and input are seen as having value.

Instead of being viewed as creating order, structure, predictability, and credibility, tradition is often viewed as the enemy. The perception of this enemy keeps me from doing what I want or what I think others should do.

In the mid-1980s the dysfunctional family was of popular concern. The traditions that bound families together were eroded. I predicted then that if we had many dysfunctional families in the 1980s, managers would probably encounter a workforce that would have trouble dealing with boundaries and differences in the 1990s.

When I was a single parent, I based my work schedule on what the boys and I wanted to do for our annual vacation. One day at the dinner table I asked the boys if they would like to go to Disneyland. "Yeah!" they replied, "that would be great!" I then determined when the Dodgers would be in town. I made my plans around those dates. I was able to get work in Southern California, to see Mom and Dad, go to Disneyland, and see the Dodgers play. It became a tradition for us to do something like this every year. When Becky and her son, Doug, became members of our family, neither knew very much about sports. During the past five-and-one-half years, Becky has seen more sporting events than at any other time in her life. She has become a super sports mom and a play-by-play announcer for me.

Here is an example of her play-by-play description of one of Neil's basketball games: "John Miller inbounds the ball to Neil. Neil dribbles the ball up the court and across the time line. He hurls the ball over the corner to Toogood. Toogood shoots, he biffs!" Becky knew nothing about sports until she met me. She had to become familiar with something that is traditional for me — my love of sports. She was willing to change and adapt her schedule and her life to mine. For my part, I don't watch sports as much as I used to. Each of us has adapted to change, to the new relationship.

If groups of people are going to get along and meet corporate goals, we must learn how to adapt to change while also respecting the fact that we come from different backgrounds.

There also are times when we must adapt to changing situations beyond our control. In many of my workshops I talk about the phases most of us go through in adapting to necessary change.

I. Grief and Loss

It is necessary to deal with reality when things are changing so fast that we barely have time to know what's happening. Technology, work assignments, and demographics are undergoing rapid change. Some people are having to learn for the first time how to work with the opposite gender or a person of color.

Those of us who are creatures of habit become accustomed to working with the same type of people doing the same type of thing, telling the same kind of jokes. The loss we may feel is about not having things be the way they once were. As time passes, things that were problems take on sentimental meaning. We forget the pain and struggle. We just remember how it was before.

2 Fear and Resistance

One of my colleagues, Will Schultz, says that anger and fear are rarely the first reactions we have to change. The real frustration is the loss of control. Most of us do not like to be told what to do. We like to make our own decisions. When a parent or manager makes a decision that we don't like, we become resistant.

In the introduction to this book, I speak of the importance of core values. I think the four core values driving workplace behavior today come under the heading of safety: physical safety, political safety, spiritual safety, and emotional safety.

I have been in two workplaces where there have been physical violence. Employees and children are afraid of having their roots pulled out by mergers, divorces, and the like. Some children are numb to change. They don't know to feel fear because there were no roots in the first place.

When people show fear, they may ask many questions. They may not want answers. They may be telling us by their questions that they do not like what is being presented. Do not believe that all questions are efforts to seek clarification or knowledge. Certainly we do need to ask questions, but it has been my experience that when many questions surround a particular incident or topic, people are really trying to make a statement. Sometimes I will ask a person to tell me what is behind the question. That person is then freed up to give me their statement or opinion.

3. Excitement and Anticipation

During this phase, people become excited because they have some control about how and what change will look like. It takes a wise person who can say, "In the midst of an unanticipated moment, what can I learn from this experience?"

Examples of anticipation and excitement might be a pending marriage or a new job. Yet, we experience grief and loss as well as fear and resistance before we reach excitement and anticipation phase.

As difficult as it was for me to go to the School for the Blind, I grew there and became a strong, well-rounded individual who learned how to read and write and even to have some fun.

As I'm writing this chapter, I'm planning a reunion with four of my closest friends from that school. Some of us have not seen one another for thirty-five years. What I learned at the school has made it possible for me to live a productive life today. I have my parents to thank for the foresight and courage to send me to school even though it was hard for all of us.

4. Organizational and Cultural Change

Becky, Doug, Neil, Erik and I met as individuals. Today, we continue to create a new culture. Each of us is better individually as a result of that change. How do I know? We don't always see the benefits of the change we implement until years later. That is a problem for us in the United States, because we are such a "me, me, me" society that emphasizes instant gratification.

Paul Stookey of Peter, Paul, and Mary said that we can sometimes measure change by the literature we read. In the 1950s we read *Life* magazine; in the 1960s it was *People*; in the 1970s, *Us*; in the 1980s we read *Self*, and in the 1990s we read *Me*. These magazines reflect change in emphasis.

When corporations hire me today, they want instant results. Sometimes they want my training class of one-and-one-half days or a one-day session to "fix" their problems. What they really need are up to three years of ongoing consulting or coaching preceded by sessions on visioning and strategic planning.

Deeply embedded in the Japanese culture is a one-hundred-year vision. I have heard that the leaders in Japan have a vision starting with their children and continuing all the way to their great-great- grandchildren. If our vision extends that far out, we will not see instant results.

John C. Maxwell invites us to examine three dynamics when we talk about change.

1. People do not change until it hurts enough

Until legislation outlawed workplace discrimination on

the basis of race, gender, or ethnic background, hiring practices did not change. And yet the laws that we made have
become scapegoats for a perception on the part of some that
women and people of color only get the job because of the
law, not because they are qualified. In some cases, earlier on,
there may have been preferential hiring. Fear and resistance
may have had something to do with that.

I get nervous when it comes time to go to the dentist. I
avoid it for as long as I can. One time the dentist had to do
a root canal on the spot. From that day forward I have
become very disciplined about making sure I get checked
either annually or biannually. I don't ever want to hurt like
that again. This is a dramatic change for me. I want to pre-
vent pain if at all possible.

2. The approach

It is easy to set a goal and an approach. Sometimes, however, it may become necessary to change the route to the
goal. It is the approach that becomes the potential source of
conflict. Individuals may even believe they are arguing about
different goals. Where the approach becomes clear is when
we are on the highway and see a detour sign. The goal is still
the same but the way to get there is changed. I was inter-
viewing to join a mental health group that consisted of psy-
chiatrists, psychologists, social workers, and counselors.
One of the interview questions was, "What are your goals
and what is your timetable?" The question startled me for a
moment because I made a quick discovery while recovering
from the initial shock of the question.

"My goal is to become a private practitioner," I replied. "I am one year late in working toward this goal because my father-in-law is dying of cancer and my wife and I spend most of our available time going to be with him and my mother-in-law." As I spoke those words, I found myself able to free myself from previous negative feelings about not having attained my goal more quickly. The goal of getting into private practice hadn't changed, but my timing and approach had to take a detour.

3. We must equip people to make changes

Recently, I submitted a proposal to do work with a government agency on how to deal with change. The agency is going through a major downsizing due to a defeated tax levy. One of the impressive qualities about that proposal was the attention being given to the people who are left behind. The agency wanted to assist managers in breaking the bad news, work with the employees who were being laid off, and help the employees who were going to remain in the workplace. Each group would need help in dealing with the change process. Each individual in each one of those groups would go through their own version of grief and loss, fear and resistance, and they would also have to deal with a cultural shift.

We have traveled a long way from being creatures of habit. The need to embrace the change process means that we are constantly evaluating how we deal with things of the past and letting go of the past. As we let go, we are able to retain those elements that give us a strong frame or character of who we can become.

It is with sadness that I write this: In many cases I work with a group of people who while growing up did not receive the strong grounding that I feel I have. I work hard to maintain those elements of my early upbringing that will help me live here now and in the future. I hope that I will be able to leave my children with a legacy. As Becky and I work through the family blending part of our journey, I am struck by how we were unable to maintain a constant tradition for our boys, especially throughout the holiday season. That is where many of my memories of tradition are still very strong.

What I do know is that I want to hang onto what is important to me, but only two things are permanent. One is change, and it is a part of the process. The second is that I have eternal life with God. To me this means that any earthly tradition or material good will not last.

I like to think of myself as an open, growing individual. I must tell the truth, though. There are things I hold onto still. Sometimes I hold onto them too tightly.

Once in the midst of the 1960s when many of us were espousing openness, I went home to visit my parents. I had just graduated with a master's degree and had learned all the tools for being open with others. I had learned that I must be open to change. As soon as I walked in the door, however, I got mad at my parents for moving a particular chair.

Why was I mad? Because the location of that chair was something I could count on as a creature of habit. I always went to that chair.

We all need something we can count on to ground us. When that something is changed, we tend to be thrown off, to put down others for making the changes they want to make, especially when they inconvenience us personally.

There are no set rules anymore. We as authority figures have lost the respect of our youth and employee groups.

What can we do to get that back? What must we do to find and or create a life or character that we may never have known before? I am not saying I have all the answers, but I believe there are approaches that can help us come together again.

CHAPTER 6

Loving, Listening, and Believing

ONE OF THE GAMES WE PLAY WHILE I AM AT the School for the Blind is police force. I really like that game because I am always the captain. As captain, I rule over all the other boys. We are committed to being the biggest, strongest, and best police in America. We stand for bringing law and order to the public, and we will go to any means to get it done. We are powerful, and there is no stopping us.

We play the game every day for two years straight.

I like my role because not only does the public respond to me and feel grateful for my services, but the people who work under me do as well. Whatever I say needs to be done is done. Any idea that come from me is implemented.

And now, today, I wonder where that child's sense of

power came from? I'm wondering if, as an adult, I would ever want people to jump at my every command? There is no growth for them or for me in that kind of dynamic. Actually, it is through learning from and sharing with others that we really grow.

As I think back upon this boyhood game of police force, I continue to be fascinated by trying to define what it means to be powerful. Power, to me, in those days was equated with brute strength and force. Where did that perception come from?

Our role models in the radio programs we listened to were powerful. Later, my television heroes were Matt Dillon, a United States Marshall, and Cheyenne Bodie, a rough and tough frontier scout, who said little but maintained law and order.

Our role models were powerful authority figures we could trust. It was a time when high value was placed on family unity. Though I learned my family values from personal experience, I was also aware of the media contribution.

Our television role models were the all-American families in The Adventures of Ozzie and Harriet, Leave It to Beaver, The Donna Reed Show, and Father Knows Best.

But the role models we viewed on television seemed sometimes to conflict with the lives we lived. Definitions were in flux. As late as the early 1990s I discovered a new definition of power from Thomas Crum, author of The Magic of Conflict. He defined power as the "ebb and flow of energy unrestricted enroute to your intended goal." This was a definition that allowed individuals access to power without exerting power over someone else.

I can see that in my youth I learned to place high values on power and family. But power today seems to have its source in energy rather than brute force.

And yet maintaining law and order is important. Laws are needed to preserve order. Order is important because people need to feel safe. Whether adults, adolescents, or children, people no longer seem to feel safe in today's world.

As I write this chapter, I am deeply concerned about the erosion of law and order and family. I wonder why people seem to feel lost, to feel unsafe rather than protected.

In the 1960s, a new generation of young people began to question everything we stood for. It seemed to us that integrity had vanished, that hypocrisy was everywhere. And so we questioned authority. We wouldn't do exactly what we were told to do.

In response, corporations introduced revolutionary concepts in the workplace. One was participatory management, which sought input and involvement from employees rather than giving them directives. Among the changes, corporate groups sponsored encounter groups to find out how you felt.

In 1967, I was on Sunset Boulevard in Los Angeles, where I met a young woman who was stoned on drugs. I asked her why she wanted to do that.

"See up there?" she asked, pointing toward Beverly Hills. "That's where my parents live. They have more alcohol in their house and more medicine in their cabinets than you can imagine, but they tell me not to do drugs. They are hypocrites."

I will never forget that encounter because this young woman was blaming her parents for judging her by one set of standards, yet living by another.

I realized that the "have nots" of the world resent the "haves'" authoritative perspective. That is, the "have nots" feel the "haves'" hypocritical message is, "You can have what I have as long as I need not give it up."

Over the years, this two-level existence has eroded appreciation of authority figures of many kinds.

Children do not always appreciate their parents; the nonbeliever does not always appreciate the doctrines or judgments of Christians, and clients of rehabilitation agencies do not always appreciate the services they receive from government agencies whose existence is designed to help the clients become employed.

This latter category took on particular significance for me when I moved to Portland to become director of the Client Assistance Project for the State of Oregon's Commission for the Blind. We in this federally funded project served as advocates for clients who had become dissatisfied with service delivery or had experienced delays in service to blind people.

The question gnawing at my gut was why do people who want to help other people become unappreciated? Why is there this dynamic where we give our heart and soul to help someone, and yet instead of appreciation, we get an angry response?

In a systemic context, we sometimes find dedicated people willing to serve, but who unknowingly undermine the integrity of the people they want to help. For instance, clients may believe the person helping them is speaking condescendingly. Eventually, the client refuses help rather than be talked down to.

Of course, not everyone has others' interests at heart. I'm talking about those who are trying to do it right — the parents, the managers. I am also thinking about people who are struggling to get employees or others for whom they are an authority figure to follow their directives.

Many of my blind clients didn't appreciate the help being given to them. On the other hand, vocational rehabilitation counselors realized there was a discrepancy between what the clients knew about themselves and what the agency people knew about them. The agency knew the client's name, social security number, and desired occupation or dream. But the client did not feel that the helping agency believed in the integrity of his or her dreams. There was a gap between dreams and practicality.

I began to see a connection between the client group and children who feel thwarted by parents, though for the most part the parents love them deeply. It is the adolescent push-back or that behavior which resists a person or group in a position of authority. Usually the authority figure provides comfort, shelter, or some other type of support. Nevertheless, the child, employee, or client resists the support. Contributing to this pushback is a premature desire to be independent. It is critical for the person in authority to work hard to maintain the integrity of the individual or group we are striving to help. Sometimes a great mandate goes awry because of the manner in which the message is delivered. We must be able to put our own biases or desires aside to preserve the integrity of the person we are trying to help or have responsibility for.

Adolescent pushback has a systemic dynamic because groups of people are now resisting or pushing back against other groups who are in positions of authority.

This is a very complex issue. I will try to break it down into some understandable pieces.

I. Structure and Freedom

We must look first at the difference between freedom and structure. I once thought that when I grew up I would be free to do whatever I wanted. At twelve, I could hardly wait until I was forty or fifty because then nobody could tell me what to do.

We need a certain amount of structure before we can obtain true freedom, however. Authority, law, or powerful people historically create structures for people to live by or under. Such structure may be missing an ingredient or core value like treating people with respect and integrity.

I was raised to respect my elders and to do as I was told. Today I go around the country teaching people how to respect each other. I probably confused respect with obedience during my early years. Part of that is due to my cultural upbringing. You probably were brought up with a similar mind-set if you are over the age of fifty.

To me, integrity means that we do what we say we are going to do. We are accountable for our actions. Too many promises broken by authority figures have eroded this core value. If there is no respect or integrity in place, structure is destined to fail.

II. Belief or Nonbelief

Once, during a conversation among counselors at the Commission for the Blind, one of us said, "A regular guy would be able to go out and do this job." Instantly we stopped. What?

We wanted our clients to succeed, yet sent the message to them that they were not, "regular guys."

How could they become successful if we didn't believe that they could become successful? It was a subtle message that our clients were picking up from us.

How could I fall into that way of thinking since I am blind myself? The answer is simple. I did not think of myself as a regular person. Regular people could see. Regular people could do.

So there I was, thinking like a "have not." It is a secondary or subservient position comparable to the positions of women to men, children to parents, or employees to employers. It is the "haves" and "have nots" conversation.

III. Values Drive What We Do

What are the core values that really drive the action we take? If one of our core values is that we are not as good as the other person, it will hamper our ability to be out there striving for our intended goal. Our energy will not have ebb and flow and will be very restricted.

In 1997, I presented to my colleagues in cultural diversity a paper with social, political, and moral implications. The paper brought my faith in Jesus Christ to the table for discussion in addition to a curriculum item on sexual orientation.

I did not want to get into a discussion of whether or not the gay/lesbian curriculum should or should not be in the workplace. I *did* want to introduce Christianity to the conversation, since this was the group that was being criticized for their lack of attentiveness to gay/lesbian people.

I wanted my colleagues to see how having a personal relationship with Jesus Christ was different from the judgmental or hypocritical behavior of Christians around the subject of laws and doctrines.

I am writing to those authority figures who unintentionally convey messages they do not mean to convey. Example: "Blind people are not regular people." This message is counterproductive to our believing we can develop the necessary skills to reach our dreams. The same is true for us as parents or as managers of employees.

There are two models of authority. The difference between the two is in how instructions are given. In the non-productive model, instructions are given in a manner that is judgmental, demeaning, and punitive. In the productive model, instructions are given with respect, patience, and discernment. What do we mean by this? Respect, I have found, needs to be earned. We have often said that children or employees need to earn our respect. I think just the opposite is true. When I shared my faith with my diversity colleagues, I was totally received. They didn't become converted to follow Jesus, but they listened with interest and in some cases were touched by what I had to say. What I had to say was free of treating them judgmentally and free from demeaning them for making different choices. They met me for who I am as a person, a fellow human being on this earth. Discernment is timing. It is when, how, and who delivers the message you want to convey. Timing is everything. Timing can only have true impact when a relationship is established. In our attempts to get our point of view across to people, we may be smothering them instead.

When we act with respect, patience, and discernment, we form genuine relationships.

I find that in forming relationships, what the other person wants to know from me is am I for real? That is, will I do what I say I'm going to do.

In families, children need consistent love. Even when they make mistakes, they need to know of our abiding love. We need to restore the value of love into our way of being. This applies even in the workplace. I once thought that respect preceded love, but I have shifted my thinking.

IV. Discipline and Focus

One of the most heralded coaches in football, Vince Lombardi, had a true love for his players. It was through his love for his players that he was able to maximize the performance of each individual on the team.

Those who know Lombardi also know that he was one of the most disciplined and focused men in the game. Once, after a loss, he took his team back to the locker room, drew an oblong shape on the blackboard, and said, "Gentlemen, this is a football."

In other words, the team had poorly executed the fundamentals in their game plan. Lombardi exercised discipline and focus to make his point, and he made it with authenticity because he had formed a genuine relationship with his players. Team players need to appreciate authenticity in relationships in order to receive direction and do what we want them to do even if they do not want to do it.

The first underpinning of relationship formation for each of us is to become our own unique individual. The second underpinning to relationship formation is the need to belong. The need for acceptance or approval is higher for some people than for others. These two underpinnings set the stage for how and why tension arises between the "haves" and the "have nots."

It is the responsibility of leaders, managers, coaches, or parents to create the environment in which others will respond to them. Vince Lombardi created an environment of discipline and focus.

V. Control and Fear

Both "haves" and "have nots" are susceptible to loss of control, fear, and doubt. Those in power either do not want to lose control or they fear having to do something different because they may lose rank, possession, or esteem. Doubt sets in around the issue of how to accommodate someone's needs. Such accommodation may require doing something different.

The "have nots" want to obtain some control in their lives. Those who are deprived in simple things will often strike out to do anything to obtain some form of identity. They want to be successful but doubt whether they can really succeed. Sometimes parents, agency people, or school officials read this lack of performance as poor motivation. What is really happening is that doubt has set in.

All of us have access to some kind of power. How we use it is either constructive or destructive. Power or the need to have it may be driven by the need to be seen as unique or the need to belong. The implications of this need depend on how much or how little people feel respected, treated with integrity, and receiving of proper guidance and direction.

When I shared my paper on morals in the workplace with a group of leading diversity consultants, I learned three very important things:

First, we need to earn the right to be heard. Through my day-to-day and in some instances year-to-year work with these consultants, I have established myself as someone they could respect. We need not agree in approach or action, but we must share respect for one another's talents, gifts, and characteristics.

Second, my colleagues resented the hypocrisy that is evidenced by many Christians. We promote the gospel of Jesus Christ and then become judgmental if someone does not meet our standards.

For example, in the workplace, some companies have family benefits written in such a way that people who are not married are not covered. The issue is not whether or not I agree with that policy but how I treat people whose lifestyles differ from mine. Jesus was among all the people, the poor, the depraved, and the sick.

Finally, legalism and doctrine should not be confused with teaching people to abide by what is expected. Even when we must discipline someone for inappropriate activity, their integrity must be kept intact.

During the search for uniqueness, an individual may need to wander, flounder, and fail. Christians and parents find it difficult to allow nonbelievers or their children to do this. During the dark hours, we must still be with those we care about. Development of uniqueness comes only when we are lost. Through our search, we can come closer to God or withdraw from Him. Being lost should not be confused with allowing someone to walk into a situation where they would be destroyed.

Character assassinations are not appropriate at any level.

When I think about the many times I have made mistakes, I am ever thankful for God's patience with me. Patience is harder for some of us to exercise when we see someone we care about do something that is either wrong or inappropriate. During the search for uniqueness we may only be able to be a listener and to convey to that person that he or she matters. What is wanted during this time is validation.

In the workplace, we may need to limit the wandering, floundering, and failure, but we can hold a person's integrity intact.

Romans 12:2 says "… be transformed by the renewal of your mind." In some cases transformation needs to be preceded by reformation. In situations where people have exceeded the boundaries of appropriate behavior, we need to reform how we build relationships. Love must be the precursor to building respect. Love is based on believing in someone when they do not believe in themselves. The process is to love, listen, and believe.

In addition, we must be authentic, demonstrate respect, become disciplined, and stay focused on our goals and purpose in life.

If we are a member of the "have not" community, we need to love the person who loves us, listen to the person who is speaking to us, and act on that person's belief in us when we do not believe in ourselves.

CHAPTER 7

Living and Working from Oneness

ONE EVENING, MY SON, NEIL, COMES INTO my room while I am preparing to leave on a business trip. He asks if he can stay overnight at a friend's house.

"No," I reply.

"Why?" he asks.

"Because I said so," I reply.

"Why," he asks again.

"Because I said so," I reply.

"WHY?" he asks again. This time his voice is more animated.

"BECAUSE I SAID SO," I reply with an equal amount of

animation.

This question and answer are repeated two or three times. Each time our voices rise. Suddenly I stop and think. I change course. "Hey Neil," I begin, "what's our mission?"

"Celebrate oneness," he replies reluctantly.

"Are we in our mission now?" I ask.

"No," he says.

"What needs to happen so you can be back in our mission?" I inquire.

"Stop whining," he responds.

His response brings me up short. I realize then that in my concentration on myself and on tomorrow's trip, I'm not in the mission either.

"Neil," I say, "you know what? I'm not in the mission either. Let me tell you what's going on. The reason I want you home tonight is that I am leaving tomorrow and I will be gone for one whole week. I want to spend time with you. What I need in order to be back in oneness is to be with you. Is that okay?"

Without hesitation Neil says, "Sure, Dad."

His friend has been listening to this exchange at the door to our apartment. Neil gets up, walks over to the door, and says to his friend, "My dad and I need to be together tonight, so we'll have to do our thing another time."

What had started out to be a no-win power struggle turned out to have resolution. What factors contributed to this?

We were on the wrong track from the start. First of all, a

parent should never say "because I said so." It's punitive and demeaning and probably originated with the child being taught to obey authority. But Neil and I were both off track.

I had forgotten for that moment with my son the thing I'd learned that had become my mission. When we live with and work with a mission, it is much bigger than whatever problem we may be experiencing.

Too often our problems arise from the What's-In-It-For-Me (WIIFM) principle. It can be so strong that we become oblivious to the feelings of others and don't recognize the impact we're having.

Usually, we're in a hurry. Ours is an instant gratification society. We want something or to be with someone now, not later. We want our problems fixed immediately. We fail to see how we got out of alignment with each other.

The mission to "Celebrate Oneness" came to me during a two-day workshop in which I took part with other business owners. The purpose of the workshop was to help us create something beyond ourselves. The mission had to be bigger than we would become. As participants, we were asked to identify low times in our lives and to forecast our vision for optimum performance.

Prior to the workshop, I had been convinced that my mission was to celebrate diversity. I was on the verge of becoming nationally known in this field.

But in the workshop, as questions came my way repeatedly asking what was important to me, my responses seemed to reflect the need for inclusion, belonging, harmony, and all individuals having a chance to exercise their gifts or to be who they are.

The person who was working with me asked me to visualize an ultimate experience. I chose being in an airplane soaring high above the clouds. Then she asked me to describe who was with me and what I was doing. I described being able to look down on earth and seeing different groups of people being together and yet being different. Those on the plane with me were family and friends I admired. Colleagues who were special to me were also in this group on the plane.

"This doesn't sound like diversity," said one participant listening to the questions directed at me. "It sounds like togetherness."

"What's your mission?" This final question was asked repeatedly. Then it hit me

"Celebrating oneness!" I shouted with glee. I saw it. I saw my mission was not to celebrate diversity, but to celebrate oneness.

"Are you sure?" they asked.

"Celebrating oneness," I said with as much clarity and confidence as was humanly possible.

Several life themes contributed to this declaration. First was the importance of belonging and harmony in the Japanese culture. Belonging to groups is very important to me today.

I remember walking into the snack bar as a sophomore in college. Everyone but me seemed to be engaged in conversation. Though I was known as a person who could get up and sing in front of other people, I had difficulty establishing effective one-to-one relationships.

In front of a group of people, I felt confident and in control. Not so in a personal relationship. You don't know where a one-to-one relationship will go. If I'm afraid of what you'll think or do, I'll set it up so that you can't reject me. Frankly, I was starving for acceptance and inclusion. It hurt like crazy, this anticipating rejection if I asked a girl out on a date. The sad part was that maybe she wouldn't reject me, maybe she would accept, but I wouldn't believe her because I was programmed to feel rejection, to feel lonely.

I had known what it meant to feel left out. I had felt excluded from playing baseball with friends, from Sunday school-related activities at church parties, from being able to look at pictures like sighted people.

The second dynamic that surfaced during the workshop was the realization that we are all part of the body of Christ, yet we are all different. In Romans 12, Paul tells us to live in harmony with one another. Ephesians 4 is about one body with one spirit using different gifts.

The body is that to which we belong. I learned later that the group to which I belong is not what is important. Instead, I need to be part of the body of Christ.

Those awful moments of feeling left out were gradually being replaced with the realization that I could help all people feel included, valued, and special. I work hard to make each person I meet feel that way.

It sounds idealistic and perhaps even Pollyanna-like, but it's true. I want people to know that they are valued for who they are or who they can become.

I realized that the mission, "Celebrating Oneness," could be my path toward accomplishing this objective.

There are two things that make a mission successful. First, a mission provides you with a sense of being grounded, centered, and focused. It establishes a place you work from, not toward. This is very important to understand.

When Neil and I were at odds with one another, we were each working toward something. He was working toward the goal of staying overnight, while I was working toward the goal of having him stay home. Being grounded in the mission of oneness helped us unlock the conflict and refocus on what we are in relationship to one another.

The mission of oneness is biblical in that we are all parts of the body of Christ.

Our mission is our root structure. My roots are in a strong family of Japanese heritage. I grew up with a set of values that are important to me, and, of course, my real center now is in my relationship with Jesus Christ.

The second thing that a mission does is to help us get beyond the confines of yourself. No longer are we wrapped up exclusively in our dreams, our conflicts. We can have an impact on other people. We have the opportunity to transform our family, workplace, industry, and the world in which we live.

Celebrating oneness has become a trademark for me

among my diversity colleagues. It is what I believe makes me unique.

One of my clients asked what I did to get corporate officers to respond. "It's not anything I do," I said, "It is who I am." The importance of a diversity initiative in the workplace is not about what we do initially; it is about who we are and what we stand for. The next step is to look at tools for implementation.

Oneness provides us with a place to stand and work from in times of dreaming and in times of crisis. It also means each person can have a different set of actions to help them be in oneness.

Oneness means developing individuals and organizations to reach their highest potential. I work from the place of being centered in myself and with God. I work toward connecting with others, whether it be at home or on the job. Once the mission is established, we are given the necessary tools and led in the direction we need to go.

One of the challenges is that you and I may have different definitions of oneness or we may even differ on what needs to happen so that we can be in oneness.

I am in oneness when I am at Dodger Stadium, eating a hot dog and peanuts, and listening to the golden voice of Vin Scully giving a play-by-play description of the game.

Becky, on the other hand, thinks that watching a baseball game is as interesting as watching grass grow. Baseball is the farthest thing from her mind in terms of oneness.

I want to introduce four concepts to help us understand

what is happening when we do not experience oneness. We can use them to build some bridges between our differences so that we can more effectively learn how to be with each other.

I. Likeness

Likeness embodies attributes that are similar. I think the need to be like someone else is driven by the need to feel included, liked, or accepted. One wants to feel important, so the thing to do is to hang out with important people.

Some of us feel important if we meet movie stars or professional athletes. Others want to be on the executive board. Once we start trying to be like someone else, we risk thwarting our own potential.

To be Christlike, for example, really means to develop the gifts that God has given us. Christlikeness comes when we treat people with love and respect, appreciating each person's unique contribution.

It is false to say that all Japanese people look and speak alike or that a person from one engineering group is just like someone from another engineering group. What is false is that although they may come from similar groups, there are still inherent differences that make one person unique and unlike another.

The human eye sees only likeness. Likeness makes us fall prey to "sameness."

II. Sameness

Sameness comes out of expecting all people who are alike

to behave in the same manner. That is, we may expect all Asians to be quiet and, therefore, not made of leadership material, or we may expect all Christians to be judgmental. As the workplace changes, we must look back to the time when we wanted everyone to assimilate, to be alike, or to do the job in the same way.

Likeness and sameness have been confused with helping many people envision a goal. Instead of striving for mutual goals in the workplace, we often try to make people do the same job in the same way instead.

Sameness is conformity. Conformity puts people into boxes in which they do not fit. Sameness is the perceived order. When we want people to do everything the same way, when we level the playing field, we may also lose touch with the goal of hiring the person best qualified for the job.

III. Commonness

I have been teaching a Sunday School class on a rotating basis for the past three-and-one-half years. One Sunday — the day I met someone who became important in my life — I presented a lesson on heroes and their characteristics.

I identified Vin Scully of the Dodgers as one of my heroes. For me, Vin is a communicator who can draw word pictures, and he speaks from his heart. He knows his craft and can relate to his audience.

I did a mini play-by-play description of a baseball game in much the same way that Vin calls the action. Then I asked participants to identify their heroes.

Randy Banks, who with his wife, Mollie, had moved to our area from Texas, was visiting our class for the first time. He talked about Mickey Mantle. Since his hero Mickey Mantle had been a switch hitter, Randy had also became a switch hitter. Randy and I seemed to have interests in common. When I mentioned that I am a runner, that sealed it. Today Mollie and Randy Banks are very good friends with Becky and me. Why? Because we are alike? No, because we found some points of commonness.

Some workplaces attempt to make everyone alike. They are missing the connection. While it is true that a positive dimension of likeness can be developed if you allow the commonness to surface, it is allowing each person to be an individual while enjoying a common focus that is important.

When we take part in a common event or can delight in some other areas of commonness, we can also delight in the unique and individual contributions that each person has to offer.

This is what I believe is often missing in homes and places of work. When actions are criticized, people do not feel valued for who they are. When I talk about acceptance, please do not think I mean accepting things that are violent, deviant, or otherwise outside the law.

At this point, if you understand what commonness means, then you may want to learn about the qualities that make for effective teams, families, and communities. We really can't separate our business lives from our personal lives. That would be like taking one part of myself and putting it on ice while the other part works. I am one being. All of my parts must function at all times. These attributes, if used properly, can help individuals and groups, be in oneness.

First, create a positive and safe climate for people to be who they are and to do their jobs.

In today's society, there is a serious decline in people feeling safe or valued. We may need to create safe climates and points of commonness as well.

Second, create a common focus. Though we are different, we can succeed if we have a common understanding of the task and the approach.

Third, recognize and appreciate individual differences. This means we allow for individual differences in viewpoint and approach to a task, while keeping the person's integrity and dignity intact.

Fourth, understand the roles, responsibilities, and procedures of each person in relationship to the operational requirements of your organization or family.

Next, have strong leadership that can give and receive feedback in a loving way, be authentic, and be open to the leading and suggestions of others.

IV. Reciprocity

Reciprocity means give-and-take in a relationship. We give what we have to give and we receive what the other person has to give. If this is so simple, why, then, is there conflict?

I believe that we are now touching the core cause of so

much strife in the world. As I write this, it seems that families are disintegrating, employer-employee relationships are not very good, and many people have a dim view of our leaders in office. Businesses proclaim themselves equal opportunity employers, but many question whether God created all of us equally.

The 1964 Civil Rights Act outlawed discrimination against people based on their race, gender, or religious backgrounds. Nowhere on this earth are we made equal, but we have all been given special gifts by our Creator. The real issue is whether people have the opportunity to exercise the gifts they have been given. I wonder about efforts to equalize tasks in relationships. It seems to me there is no such thing as a fifty-fifty relationship one hundred percent of the time. Some have more than others; some give more than others. How do we evaluate either?

A few years ago, Becky and I were in Scotland, where I was consulting for a high tech firm with its home office located in California. One of the Scots' major complaints was the teleconference meeting. It was at 8 p.m. Scotland time (*11 a.m. West Coast time in the U.S.*). The employees in Scotland resented staying three hours past the end of their work day for a meeting held at the convenience of the U.S. employees.

I was able to convey this concern to the home office, which began to vary the meeting times, but they then went too far in the other direction. Workers from the home office who had children began to complain because day care wasn't open until 7 a.m. and the meeting began at 6 a.m.. The company soon discovered the art of reciprocity, where each had to give and take. Each group's needs had been acknowledged.

I have learned that when I take things too literally, I usually encounter trouble. I don't think there is such a thing as equal or fair. What we are talking about is reciprocity: give and take according to the events and circumstances surrounding the situation in question.

Fairness is not the only issue. The area to address is about taking each situation and each relationship and maximizing it.

Institutional power influences individual behaviors and responses. It is easier to negotiate or renegotiate such personal relationship issues as who does what based on accessibility or ability. In those terms, we can work out most conflicts or misunderstandings. On a large scale, on an institutional scale, for instance, we want to make sense out of the world so we can feel like we matter. On this scale, we tend to think in terms of the "haves" and "have nots," and the gap between the two groups is widening.

If we have no recourse or if institutional power has determined lending practices or access to credit, for instance, we feel shut out from the dialogue. We feel we have no personal power. We feel others have control or legalistic power over us.

As I reflect on likeness, sameness, commonness, and reciprocity, I wonder if oneness is at the root of all of them. At the heart of most of these discussions is the people's desire for harmony. They want to feel as though they are of value.

They want to belong. They also want to feel important, loved, and respected.

I continue to believe that the root of oneness is lodged in two areas: personal and institutional. When we want to work and live in oneness, the personal must be implemented in conjunction with our environment and the needs of others. When working toward agreement about what oneness looks like on a personal or institutional level, negotiation and issues of control pop up.

Institutionally and organizationally, oneness may involve issues of power and authority. Who has what authority over whom? Employees and children today say you must earn their respect. In my day, it was the other way around: We were to respect our elders and those who were in some form of authority.

When my wife wants to go shopping, I go with her. I am not a good shopper. The reason I go shopping with her is to create oneness with her. I do not do this out of a sense of obligation, though shopping is not my first choice. If I can accompany her on such an outing, I am investing in our relationship. In a like manner, she does not necessarily choose to go to baseball games with me. She does so because of my love for the game. Living and working from oneness allows us to see the bigger picture when it would be very easy to become embedded in the immediacy of the circumstances or situation. Naturally, in relationships, things do not work out smoothly all of the time. The difference is that there is a point of reference from which to work. Institutionally, the issue is one of power and control. The word *power* can have a negative connotation when the reference is to relationships between employer and employee or parents and children. Lines of authority must be made very clear, but there must also be a positive working climate for all to work together in harmony.

As I've said before, Crum defines power as the ebb and flow of energy unrestricted enroute to your intended goal. The word *unrestricted* is key here. If energy flows without restriction, then the communications process is smooth, the processes and procedures are crisp and clear, and everyone feels good about what is happening.

In my relationship with God, I fully understand that I am the junior partner. He is the senior partner and executive officer. I have been guilty of thinking of business relationships as fifty-fifty. What we need to do is to think about how all of us partner together to accomplish a specific task or how we partner to strive for a specific outcome. In this kind of partnership, it is understood that not all of us have the same amount of power, talent, or resources. We are driven by what will make us successful. There is a corporate or common goal and then there are individual goals pertaining to a particular talent or contribution that an individual might have.

Each year, our firm sponsors a running team that runs from Mt. Hood to Seaside, Oregon. There are more than eight-hundred-and-fifty teams comprised of twelve people per team. The race is one-hundred-ninety-six miles and the goal of each team is to finish the race. Individual teams vary in ability, but individual goals are based on the ability of each runner. In addition to having twelve runners, each team must supply three volunteers who will help work the course for the runners. They also must have two drivers for each van to help runners get from one position to the other. There is a lot of individual coordination required by each team, and it must be done in conjunction with the coordination of the entire race. In total, there are more than ten-thousand people involved in this event.

I love my team because we are so different. We vary in age from twenty-two to sixty-five. We have a good mix of men, women, and people of color. The goal is clear. As a team, we encourage each other, cheer for each other and for other teams as they pass us or meet us at an exchange point. We talk about how well we work together as a team.

Why do we work well together?

We have something in common, and we understand the capabilities of each person on the team. In addition, each person understands his or her role on the team. Each is committed to do his or her part to help the entire team be successful. Finally, I think strong leadership and coordination help us work well together as a team.

What I mean is that we effectively screened who could be on our team. We didn't want people to have big egos; we wanted competence and strength in each person so that each would follow through.

I kept asking, "Why does it work so well here? Why don't

we have this kind of teamwork on the job?"

Consider the following: There are no hidden agendas. Everyone is clear about the overall objectives. Prior to the event, we have a team dinner to go over the course information and other pertinent points relevant to individuals who are responsible for key legs on the course.

Individual differences and contributions are valued. We have a commitment to a common cause and a desire to have fun.

I honestly believe that it is possible to create a similar environment in our places of work. The key is a new definition of power. In many workplaces, the goal is not clear, nor is it commonly understood. There are times when differences in style, approach, and language are not valued.

Operating counter to the energy flow we are talking about is another kind of power. That power is negative or punitive. In this kind of power, we put people down, we treat others legalistically. This form of legalism sets up a right and wrong paradigm. The form of what is right is confused with the notion that we are lowering our standards. Standards and discipline are very important. The punitive power is reinforced by those who have more than those who do not. Punitive power could be defined by money, status, education, age, and size.

The ebb and flow of energy, for me, is synonymous with experiencing the Holy Spirit. I cannot explain how that works, but for me it does. I fully recognize that for those who are not Christians, there may be a different paradigm when the energy is flowing and when everything comes together, when there is more productivity that occurs in less time.

Living and working from oneness is about the process of being — being who we are with the opportunity to utilize our talents and gifts.

CHAPTER 8

Acting Like Champions

I AM IRRITATED. AS I BOARD THE PLANE, I continue to think about the announcements I've just heard. Flight plans have changed. We are to stop in New Orleans to refuel before going on to Salt Lake City. Why didn't they plan for this? We were supposed to fly directly from Orlando to Salt Lake City, where I will change planes to get to Portland. Now I will miss my connecting flight.

I am thinking about how to find lodging in Salt Lake City, how to negotiate another flight on a different carrier, and how the airline should pay my hotel bill.

I am thinking that I'm entitled to preferential treatment. Being such a good customer, I help the airline thrive. As I sit down, I go on and on in this vein for some time. In my mind, the situation gets worse and worse until, suddenly, out of the blue, my thoughts veer elsewhere.

Who are you anyway, I ask myself? Preferential treatment indeed. Don't you remember when you criticized anyone in first class? Have you forgotten to be thankful that you're alive, that you'll get home safely, that you have a family who loves you and who is waiting for you at home?

In my work, I have seen many people get stuck believing they are entitled to certain rights, privileges, and treatments. Sometimes we confuse basic rights with the notion of entitlement. I know that I have done so myself.

On the plane, for instance, I have fallen into the trap of believing I am entitled to certain privileges just because I have acquired a certain status as a valuable customer.

And now, as I am sitting on the plane, I ask for God's forgiveness. Yes, I am frustrated because I will get home a day later than I'd planned. Yes, I think the airline should have planned better. Yes, I may not fly this carrier in the future.

Is my experience any different from what happens to any traveler who comes upon a "Detour" sign? Is my experience any different from those who get caught in traffic jams and arrive home late?

Often, we are called upon to adapt to whatever changes come our way. The true demonstration of character comes when you see how people deal with adversity.

Pat Riley, in his book, *Team Play*, talks about the demise of the Lakers in the 1980s. He believes that the downfall came about after the team values that had helped them on and off the court began to crack.

I find myself thinking now about the difference between victors and champions.

Those who are victorious in a contest win. On the other hand, champions demonstrate a certain behavior over a period of time. They are not rated exclusively by whether they win the contest or get the sale, but are measured also on their character and on how they conduct themselves over a period of time. Championship is a state of being. It represents how to be with yourself and others.

A victor wins the contest. A champion may lose the contest, but the likelihood of getting to the top is greater for the champion.

Hanamura Consulting has core values that drive how our firm does business. The values are inclusion, respect, integrity, harmony, recognition of the need to belong, family, love, and belief in God.

One of my core values, respect, had a crack at one time. I put myself above others while trying to determine how and what kind of treatment and or service I should receive. This does not mean I can't feel frustrated, but it does mean I needed to think about my values.

Values frame what we do. Some get in the way of our being at our best. If a core value is flawed by greed or the need to be right, the need for safety can become a driving force in corporate or family behavior. These values can influence how well people work together.

I want to be very careful not to imply that the core values

I listed for me and my firm are meant to be the values you should subscribe to. What I am saying, is that it is very important for any group—family, church, or corporation—to establish a set of declared values. If we have declared values, we can always get back on track when we begin to lose our way.

Champions live by their values. Here are some championship qualities that are worth examining: discipline, focus, and persevering through adversity. To be a champion, we must have discipline about who we are, what we do, and how we reach our intended goal. Champions understand that at times they may need to sacrifice personal needs or wants in order to achieve the desired outcome.

The need to be in bed at a certain time, instead of socializing with friends before a major event is an example that comes to mind for those of us in sports.

The second attribute of a champion is focus. Discipline comes more easily if we have focus. We can ask ourselves, what we are trying to accomplish. What tools or resources do we need to stay focused? What is required of us personally?

The year the Oakland Raiders played the Philadelphia Eagles in the Super Bowl there appeared to be two different standards for how teams should behave the night before the game. The Eagles had a specific bedtime. It seemed incredible that adults needed a rigid curfew. The Raiders, on the other hand, had no curfew, yet, in this instance, were able to win the game. What they had, however, was more focus in other areas. They also executed the right plays at the right time.

Champions know how to follow through. The opposition knew the game equally well, but failed to execute or follow the basic fundamentals that got them to the Super Bowl in the first place.

The third attribute of a champion is perseverance through adversity. We live in an extremely competitive world. In addition to the usual level of competition, we may also be fighting the devil. Those of us who are Christians are extremely vulnerable to the devil's attack. The devil does not want us to succeed in glorifying God. When under attack, we lose sight of our objective easily. In adversity, I think about people who exude championship postures in my life.

The three people who come to mind for me are Dick Layton, Stan Blinkhorn, and Jack Kiekel. Rather than identifying celebrities or actors, I find it helpful to identify champions who are close to me. I can relate to them. They don't know one another, but they do have the following qualities in common:

1. A strong love of the Lord. These gentlemen live their lives from a strong set of values that not only take them outside the boundaries of serving themselves but also to serving others.

2. They have strong families who support them.

3. They are people who believe in me. I could call on any of them day or night. When we are really

down, we need to call on a champion who is strong
and who supports us in who we are and what we're
about. These are the people who will hold us up
when we can't do it ourselves.

4. They are technically proficient in their chosen voca-
tions. We become only as good as our preparation.
Each of these men has discipline, focus, and technical competence.

5. All three are leaders. They influence the lives of
many in their respective churches, homes, and
places of work. I am not saying everyone should be
an institutional leader, but we do need to know our
sphere of influence or our ability to influence others. We must at least be aware what potential
impact we can have. It is interesting to note that the
impact we have may not be the impact we intend.
My three friends know how to encourage, make
tough decisions under fire, hold someone's hand if
need be, and remain focused on what they are
about. They may not be aware they have this influence.

6. The ability to adapt and lead change. Champions
breed organizations that have strong leaders. Leaders
must have vision and a willingness to get others to
follow. The truly great organizations have workers
who have the vision to pick the right leaders.

It is a fatal mistake to believe that when we reach the top — whether it be the top of an industry, top of our game, top of our profession, or a peak in our personal life — we will stay there. Nothing is forever except our relationship with Jesus Christ. It is the Christ-likeness that we must ultimately adopt to be true champions.

The championship attributes I have described in my friends can also be applied in an organization. A championship organization, corporation, school, or government agency has vision, a mission, values, and direction. It also has strong, focused leadership, an understanding of what each department contributes, and the ability to endure adversity and adapt to change. The organization must continually upgrade its technical and human relationship skills. Finally, a championship organization must support its staff, allow for mistakes, and redirect people.

Earlier, I illustrated what happens when there is a crack in the system. I now want to explore other dynamics that may contribute to the fall of champions.

The first is the loss of respect. Becky and I have numerous conversations about respect. I maintain that one of the reasons we have lost respect in this country is that the powers that be forgot that we must earn the respect of our employees, children, or students. What do I mean by that? I mean that we are not only experiencing a crack in core values, but we are also losing focus on who we are and how we should behave with others.

It is automatically assumed that as young people we must

respect our elders. This is far different from when I grew up. When I was growing up, I was taught how to show respect for my elders. We have today an entire generation of young people who may not know what respect is, much less how to demonstrate it.

We, as today's power, need to provide a loving atmosphere in order to rebuild that respect. I cannot believe today that I am being paid in two organizations to teach a course on respect. Where to begin, when there is so much unrest, family disintegration, and poor treatment of others? Before people can deal with the issue of respect, they need to know they themselves are valued. They do not feel valued today. Instead, people seem to feel beaten.

Even Christians have lost some of our collective focus. We do not behave as Christians. And when one person does something outside the boundaries of what is expected to be Christlike behavior, the entire group is judged and found wanting.

Here is an example. A well-known theologian became angry with the service on a flight. While sitting in first class, he had insisted on having certain foods at specific times and in a specific way. When he did not receive the service requested, he became angry with the flight attendants who were trying to serve him. Our theologian lost his focus and forgot that in order to be first, we must be last.

It is easy, when we move up the professional and economic ladder, to begin to expect that we are entitled to certain rights and privileges. What we must remember is the benefit of working hard to achieve extra benefits. In the process, if leadership and servant-hood are at the top of our championship list, some element of sacrifice must be remembered. Just because I was a champion last year after the Super Bowl does not mean I will be the champion this year. To be a champion, I must start all over the next day to acquire the same status.

I wonder what would happen if employee pay were based on team performance instead of individual merit. We promote teamwork with our words, but the behavior that is rewarded is based on individualism. The image we may want to look at first is partnerships with God and secondly, those with whom we work and live. If we choose the latter, many of us may have to change our thought processes as well as our actions.

Disenfranchised groups feel entitled to certain rights or treatment, though they may not believe in themselves enough to reach a desired outcome. It is possible that due to systemic or institutional barriers, the desired outcomes may not be achievable. Still, at a very deep level, there is the desire to work toward and accomplish the goal, but there is not the confidence needed to achieve it. Here's one example:

Many of my friends who have a disability fear getting off Social Security. They want to work and when given an opportunity to work they are delighted. At the same time, however, they wonder, "What if I don't make it through my 90-day probation? What if I lose my job?"

Since they have had very little opportunity to work and to

experience success, my friends do not believe they can be successful. After a while, we begin to think we have a right to Social Security because there is no such thing as meaningful work. Systemically, perhaps, we need gradually to reduce Social Security benefits rather than just chop them off.

We all have certain rights. We have the right of due process. If we are accused of a crime, we have the right to an attorney and the right to a trial. Furthermore, our guilt must be proven, for we are presumed innocent. In Vietnam, people are fearful of the police because in the eyes of the law, they are presumed guilty first and innocent second. We have the right to try for jobs and go to the store. The problem is that not all people have been afforded those rights historically.

At one time, the institutions of family, church, and corporations formed the foundations for security and predictability. Those entitlements in the past were things we could count on. But like roots and predictability, entitlements are gone. There is no guaranteed job after we get out of college.

In addition to talking about whether respect should be earned, Becky and I also discussed the merits of respecting the position even if we don't respect the person. I remember when I received my Masters degree. Mom and I argued about my status.

"I'm just a regular person. Don't put me on a pedestal," I said.

Then I realized she was respecting not only me but also

the position I held as teacher or instructor. Many years later I was challenged to try and respect the superintendent of a school. Hers was the worst disposition I'd seen. My son had had some things stolen on three different occasions. I tried to convey to her my feeling of dissatisfaction over being ripped off three times. I was in a disrespectful mode. I wrote a letter that got a response, but it was not the response that I wanted. If properly directed, anger and frustration can get us what we want. But we surely won't get what we want if we behave disrespectfully.

Personally, I struggle with the need to respect such large institutions as school districts, lending institutions, government agencies, or franchise boards. Their rules appear rigid. They don't seem to take into consideration individual needs or situations. What is missing is a connection by way of a relationship.

I was granted a bank loan from a major lending institution for the purpose of starting a town car service. The reason I got the loan was because I had a relationship with a very special individual within the organization. This person listened to my special needs as a customer, and together we worked out the arrangement for me to start my business. This is good. It demonstrates that leaders of today must re-establish connections with their constituents.

I tell major corporations today that the value that is driving workplace behavior is SAFETY, SAFETY, SAFETY, and SAFETY. Notice I said values that are driving the workplace behavior. I did not say those behaviors were "Declared

Values."

This is where love comes in. We need to love our people back to health. I'm not talking about romantic love or touchy feely love. I'm talking about love for humankind that truly demonstrates that all people matter.

In addition, to the declared values that I work from, I also have a set of beliefs that help me implement the values I spoke of earlier.

My first belief is that each person is special. I work to treat all people as if they matter and as if they contribute value to the world. I also believe that we are more alike than we are different. This belief drives home the point that we have things in common that will help bring us together no matter how different we are. We tend to let our differences drive wedges between us individually and corporately. In common, we share the desire to become successful, the need to be loved, the hope that our children will grow up and live safely in the world, and the desire to be valued for who we are.

My values and my beliefs drive what I do and how I make decisions. My love of God and family often dictate whether I choose to fly on Sunday in order to be ready to work for a client on Monday. There are exceptions, but for the most part, I do not allow myself to fly on Sunday. Not everyone has that option. If our employer says we must fly on Sunday for a Monday assignment, then we work to find other ways to meet our standards of worship.

In summary, champions fall when there is a cracking of

core values. When envy and jealously take over, we begin to lose focus. Champions also fall when respect dies as a value. People who do not behave with integrity, who do not honor their word, demonstrate lack of respect.

Chuck Swindol says that there are four things we can do to maintain our level of championship:

1. **Fight passivity.** I become passive when I'm afraid of what others will think. I lose the ability to be a champion because of my behavior.

2. **Communicate clearly with others.** This means we need to speak the truth. Speaking the truth constructively means developing our interpersonal skills to the fullest. Even then, we need to be discerning. We need to develop our skill for knowing what to say and when to say it.

3. **Discipline firmly.** Consistency is the missing link for most employees and kids today. We are not consistent in how we treat others. Therefore, it is hard to know what to expect or believe in.

4. **Maintain authority.** The respect for authority will return only when we learn how to be strong, effective leaders who can model championship behaviors.

CHAPTER 9

Keep the Faith

I HAVE JUST LEARNED THAT THE CAR DOOR WAS left open for more than six hours after the groceries were brought into the house. I go out to check on the car battery. I am irritated.

Our new neighbor is in his yard digging a fence post hole. As I approach the car, I can feel him watching me. His four-year-old daughter is standing with him, but I do not know that yet. I get into the car, strap on the seat belt, and put the key in the ignition. By now, all digging has stopped, and I know he is observing me. We have not officially introduced ourselves, but he knows I am blind. What can he be thinking?

Suddenly his daughter calls out, "It's all clear! You can go." I burst into laughter. It's wonderful. This little girl actually believes I am going to drive the car rather than simply to turn the key in the ignition to determine whether the battery is dead. True faith. The truth is I actually believe I can drive.

Faith in my belief will be tested on the day I can talk my wife or a friend into allowing me to do so. They will need faith as well. They must develop faith in themselves, in their ability to give me instructions in a timely manner. That's my theory, but so far I haven't been able to convince anyone to help me test it.

This chapter is about faith — what it is, where it comes from, how we react to adversity during times of struggle, and how we can live with the unknown.

Most of us live each day with unknowns, but because we are creatures of habit and have daily routines, we take for granted that we live our lives according to our faith. Those who believe in God and those who do not believe in God use faith. The believers remember this (most of the time). The nonbelievers may or may not think they are living with faith.

What is faith? Hebrews 11:1-2 define faith as the assurance of things hoped for but not yet seen. And yet faith, in and of itself, does not work unless we have envisioned what we want to accomplish. In the book of Habakkuk, we learn about a man with a burden, a vision, and prayer. The burden was something he felt strongly about. The vision provided direction. He prayed for God's help to reach that vision.

As a Christian, I have sometimes been hard on myself for not having enough faith to see me through a difficult situation. And yet I have learned that it is not how much or how little faith we have that affects the outcome; rather, it is what we do with what faith we have.

In Luke, we learn that if we have faith the size of a mustard seed we can move mountains. The implication is that we are not dependent on the supply of faith we have in us. It is how we use it that affects the outcome.

How do we practice being faithful? If we allow God to do his work, we open up the rooms of our internal house and let him in. Most of us — particularly in our worst moments — open only one room.

Six critical emotions influence our ability to draw on our faith.

The first such emotion is fear. When I am feeling this emotion, I am as far away from faith as I possibly can be. That isn't where I want to be necessarily, but chances are that I am so distraught or off balance that I just can't get myself into a faith mode.

One of the worst times for me was when I was sent to the school for the blind at the age of five. I got sick the first night. That moment shaped how I dealt later in my life with anything related to travel. While preparing to leave, I would get a nervous stomach, suffer from anxiety attacks, or fall into deep sadness because I was separating from those I love.

Many of us go into therapy to learn new ways to cope with previous life experiences that influence current day behavior. What is often left out of the therapy equation is our faith. Faith precludes fear.

1 John 4:18 explains that God's perfect love casts out all fear.

Steve Brown, a theologian, has said that when we are

experiencing trauma, it is impossible for us to pray for ourselves. It is reasonable to believe that we cannot focus cognitively to make decisions of any kind if we can't pray for ourselves. That is when we need others to surround us in prayer. We may need someone to put hands on us to produce a calming effect.

There are four kinds of fear. First is the fear of the unknown. How many people do we know who stay in a situation that is clearly not healthy for them? The main contributor to keeping people in place is their need for security. I may want to be somewhere else, but the fear of moving somewhere without a sense of security is too much to bear.

The second fear is not being liked. The fear of not being liked has on occasion kept me from speaking up for things I wanted or needed or from participating in activities. As parents, we are concerned about our children giving in to this fear and submitting to peer pressure. The fear of not being liked or acknowledged is linked to feelings of insecurity.

Third is the fear of being ostracized from the group to which we belong. Isolation is a terrible enemy. It paralyzes our faith, making it impossible for us to take the action that enables our faith to render positive results.

The fourth impact of fear is fear of failure, or of not doing something right. Ours is not a very forgiving society. People are not encouraged to make mistakes. We expect perfection, which may not be possible to achieve.

It took me a long time to realize that it is not wrong to be afraid. At one time I thought that as a Christian I couldn't or shouldn't be afraid. After all, I argued to myself, if we believe in God, we should know that everything works out all right. If we have fear, we are not strong Christians. I was wrong.

Instead, what I have learned over the years is that as humans, we may not be able to avoid being afraid. What I also know in my heart is that God does have sovereign control over everything. He is with us in every circumstance. I must take my fear to Him in prayer and release it to him before there can be movement.

My worst enemy has been the fear of fear itself. Sometimes I worry about what might happen to me instead of dealing with the thing I am afraid of. If I can get rid of the emotion, then I have only the specific thing, the reality, to be afraid of.

Another critical emotion is anger. There are different ways to deal with anger. One is to withdraw and say nothing. Another is to demonstrate our anger in rage. Both of these methods are, at best, inappropriate, but we use them as responses anyway because most of us are ill-equipped to deal with the emotion of anger. We try to regain control of something we cannot control. Sometimes the actions of others force us to deal with a situation that we cannot change. Feelings of loss or betrayal pour in. One of my colleagues, Will Schultz, has said that anger is rarely the first feeling we experience. He says it is the loss of control that upsets us the most.

Another way to deal with anger is to speak the truth. The Lord never said that we couldn't be righteously angry. After all, Jesus became angry when the Pharisees made a marketplace out of the temple, and he demonstrated his anger by overturning tables.

With all our advances in technology, we have not yet fully developed our ability to work with each other during times of conflict. What does it take to manage our anger? Repressing it or letting it out inappropriately only creates further damage to an already bad situation. When we experience fear and anger, most of us continue to try to handle the situation alone instead of seeking the Lord's help.

During my earlier years, I was angry because I couldn't play sports with my friends or read the newspaper. I did not have access to things that others did. Was I envious? Yes. Often, envy and jealousy are subtle responses to anger.

I have a friend who is still mad at God for not letting his younger brother live. His brother died of a blood disease. Can we alleviate anger or fear? Absolutely not! But we can learn to work with God and ask his help to deal with the anger and fear that is within us. He can handle it when we cannot. The key is not to allow ourselves to hang onto our anger for a long period of time. When it surfaces, we need to deal with it. If we don't know how, we need to seek counsel from others.

Yet another critical emotion is doubt. It offers an opportunity to encounter faith, which is the opposite of doubt. It has been said that when faith comes into the room, fear, anger, and doubt leave. Maxwell says that when the pressure is really on, there are five things to remember.

First, know who God is. Through constant study of His

Word, weekly worship in a local church, and fellowship with other believers, I improved my ability to deal with fear, anger, and doubt. The emotion of doubt is Satan's way of attacking us.

Second, know who you are. The more I know about myself, the better I am able to prepare myself to deal with uncertainty and conflict. I also can not only plan for the good things in life but also feel that they will happen.

Third, know the devil. When I was small, one of the things that kept me from getting closer to God was that I often felt I was being attacked by some weird spirit. I was to learn later that the devil can make you fearful, angry, and doubtful. By knowing ourselves, we know where we are vulnerable. I am vulnerable to self doubt, the need for approval, conflict, status, the need for money, and the fear of not belonging to a group. Perhaps I really mean the fear of being rejected from the group to which I belong. All of these attributes can serve as enemies if I allow them.

I know two people who know how to study the enemy.

One is Chuck Young, administrator for the Oregon Commission for the Blind. The other is Bud Hakanson, a community college president. Bud hired me to work at Lane Community College in Eugene. Both Young and Hakanson have an uncanny knack for determining what the enemy's strategies are and developing their approach based on this knowledge. They understand political behavior, the importance of listening to dissatisfied consumers, and the need to exercise incredible amounts of commitment to the constituencies they serve.

I need to apply this knowledge to myself when dealing with the enemy, the devil. I now know when I am vulnerable. In order to keep from falling into traps, I need to strengthen my discipline for studying God's Word; be around other people who are believers; seek counsel, advice, and encouragement from others; and keep on the path to living my faith.

Know that you are never alone. During the earlier years at the California School for the Blind, I thought I was alone. Later, when I was going through my divorce, I knew I wasn't alone. This knowledge made an incredible difference in how I dealt with daily life and, more importantly, my outlook for the future. While it is true that all of us experience individual solitude, there can be a deeper sense of calmness, peace, and joy from within that only comes when we are in touch with the Holy Spirit.

Only recently have I learned how to be alone with myself. Previously, I was so afraid of being alone that I would sometimes compromise myself in what I wanted to do or in what I wanted to say to others. When my relationship is right with God I am able to withstand being alone. This does not mean that there won't be moments of loneliness, or that we will miss being around people that we love. We will feel loneliness, conflict, frustration, but these feelings need not dominate our lives.

Finally, understand that it's okay to suffer. Who paid the ultimate price? It was our Lord Jesus Christ when He died on the cross for our sins. Suffering is a trial. Some sufferings are short-term; others are lifelong afflictions.

In the opening chapter of James, we are encouraged to count all of our trials as joy. Does that mean we like to suffer? By no means. But suffering is our teacher. It teaches us humility, compassion, and appreciation for how others feel. It strengthens our character.

Another critical emotion is joy. When I was a child, I fantasized about the day I'd grow up, get married, get a job, and live in the same neighborhood with all my friends and family. That was the ultimate. As a working person, I would be important and lots of people would love me. I could read the sports page, go to ball games, meet famous people, and maybe become famous myself. What I have learned is that those aspirations were not measures of joy, but of happiness. Someone once told me that the more we seek happiness, the more elusive it becomes.

Joy is different. Joy is the measure of how we live our faith during good times and during times of adversity and turbulence. I have often maintained that some of the crises I have experienced were not crises, but were difficulties instead. In crisis, we strengthen faith and learn how to live and be in the world. During my days as a single parent, when money was tight and I was responsible for getting the boys to their respective school events, I learned about joy and humility, which comes when you have to ask for help and don't want to.

I was forced to ask for help because I had two people that I loved and needed to care for. I learned to forfeit my pride to see that they were cared for at all costs. The greatest cost for me was my ego.

One time, my son Erik had to get to a Babe Ruth baseball game. I found someone to give us a ride to the game but had no idea how we would get home. The game location was in a secluded area where there were no major shopping stores or phones. As the game progressed, I became distracted, wondering how I'd get us home. In the top of the fifth inning, one of the parents from our team came up to talk with me. I was in the first year of the consulting firm. She asked about the firm, and I asked her for a ride home. In learning how to receive from others, God gives back. The parent later hired me to do some work in team building.

There is joy in the midst of trial, though we must open ourselves up in order to reach a deeper level of knowing who God is and who we are. We must allow ourselves the privilege of letting God serve us through others in ways that you may never imagine. Most of us live so that efficiency, self-sufficiency, and individuality prevail.

Perhaps the most humbling experience I had during my times of financial challenges occurred when a family who attended my church gave us money. Bob and Louise Meeks and their two children had planned to take a ski trip. They had saved their money. When they learned of the difficulty I was having, they held a family council meeting to discuss whether or not they should go or give their money to me. The decision was unanimous. They were going to cancel their ski trip and give their money to us.

I couldn't believe it! I didn't want to take their money, but they insisted. You see, they were teaching me that in the midst of most circumstances that are hard, there can be joy. I would have hurt them deeply if I turned the money away.

How could I not have faith, when God was providing me with experiences in my personal life that reinforced my faith? Somewhere, somehow, our places of work are also longing for something more than tangible results. The requests for team building, continuous improvement, and total quality management are attempts to say, "we need a better workplace." One thing that could help all of that is a discussion of how our belief in God could help us overcome any workplace obstacle we might experience.

One night, while getting ready for bed, we heard a knock at the door. It was Chris from downstairs.

"Do you have two pieces of bread and some baloney," he asked? "We don't have anything to eat." I was blown away. Even during my worst times financially I always had something to eat. We, of course, gave this boy what he had requested, and I also realized that my time in the apartment was a time to minister, to be a shining light to others. We helped one another, particularly as parents who watched each other's children. God provided, and there was much joy in this part of the journey.

Another critical emotion is peace. In good times and bad, there are moments when we feel peace and are well on our way to living our faith. In 1997 I experienced a difficult year in our business. I have also been experiencing the transition pains of seeing our children grow into young men. This is a joyous time in life with much to look forward to for Becky and me. However, we also have felt the effects of loss and change. One major difference, though, is that when I discipline myself to pray and read scripture, I can on some days experience an incredible peace. Children are born, provide challenges, and then are given their wings to soar. A spouse may disappoint us. Work contracts come and go. There may even be the loss of a job. But divine peace is that point in a day when our conflict or adversity may not go away immediately, but we actually become refreshed so that we can then return to the battle of life.

During the writing of this book I began a new business, a town car service of my own. I didn't know if this business would make it or not. I was confronted by the need to raise the cash to stay alive while we get this business off the ground. Despite many uncertainties, however, I found moments of truth and peace when I stepped outside of my involvements.

The books of Proverbs and Ecclesiastes help us understand how to handle life's circumstances. They provide us with the lesson of learning wisdom, of learning that everything in life is meaningless. The context of that statement is that when we are born, we come into the world with nothing but ourselves. When we die, we leave the world with nothing but ourselves. When people tell us to lighten up, they may be right. Is it possible to take ourselves too seriously? Peace comes in knowing that while we are here on earth, all things and activities we are involved with are temporary. I strive to be good at what I am involved in — my work, family relationships, and church activities. In the end, though, none of it will matter, and we come face to face with our eternity.

I think that the encounter with our Creator occurs when we face the worst about ourselves — that is, the true unworthiness of who we are. I have come to grips with my inadequacies. I don't always like myself and my limitations. When I can experience peace in spite of those infirmities, then I can be about the business of living my faith. I learn to rely on others for their help, encouragement, and support. I understand that no accomplishment on my part is done by myself.

The final critical emotion is love. Love is unconditional from God. He loved us enough to give us His one and only Son so that we could have eternal life (see John 3:16). Although love comes to us in the person of Jesus Christ, it also must come from those we work and live with. We all have the opportunity to become Christlike.

What does that mean? It means that to be Christlike is to be accepting of others, to appreciate their differences, and to convey to them a sense of their importance. We have put so many conditions on the term love. Love is romantic, erotic, parental, brotherly, sisterly, or that of a friend. I am not an expert on love, but when I read and pray, I begin to understand what true love can be.

Love is the ingredient that is missing from most of our relationships. It is missing when people are no longer respected for their positions, when children and young people don't respect their parents, when many do not believe in the church or its pastors.

What must we do to regain love? When it is present, love truly allows others to be who they are. I do not mean that love is total acceptance with no boundaries or standards. But I do mean that love serves as the foundation from which our faith grows and becomes actively alive for us and for those whose lives we touch.

Here are the three basic belief systems for how to live our faith:

1. God loves us. This love is unconditional and is available to anyone who will accept His Son as Lord and Savior.

2. Anything is possible. When we begin to pray in the midst of a difficult circumstance, we must believe that anything is possible. We may or may not get what we seek, but the possibility is there.

3. All things work together for the total good for those who are called to His purpose (see Romans 8:28). This does not mean that everything in life is good, but that good can come from what happens if we ask the basic question, "What can I learn from this experience?" I argue strongly that beliefs drive behavior. For me, these three beliefs serve as the backdrop for determining how we can truly live our faith to the maximum.

I now want to introduce the attributes of what it takes to live our faith. They are *believing, expecting, and waiting.*

Believing in someone or something is the first step in

operationalizing your faith. Do we or do we not believe in God? Some people say, "I'll believe it when I see it."

Believing in God means that we start with the unseen. The unseen becomes tangible when a vision is created to make it become seeable to us humans.

Once I believe in God, I can begin to look at what I must experience to let me know that I believe in my own capabilities. Our faith is really put to the test when we experience adversity.

I would like to mention a few people who have believed in me during critical times in my life. It is impossible to mention everyone, but the people I'm going to talk about are individuals who stood with me and behind me when it was hard for me to believe in myself.

The first person is Jean Nilsen. I met Jean in the mid-1980s. She provides ministry in healing and renewal. I have heard that repentance means you need to change direction, and I needed a change of direction. My original purpose in going to her was to pray for healing of my eyesight. I wrote at the onset of this book that I began my consulting firm to prove that I could make it despite my blindness. I wanted to see in order to become more independent, drive a car, see the faces of my children, and participate in sporting events. From the age of seven to nine I prayed for sight every night. Most of my life I've gone to church. I believed that God could heal me, but He didn't want to. When I started my work with Jean, I soon learned how rigid I was (and still am) in some instances. I began to understand that the healing that needed to take place had to come from inside and not outside. Little did I realize at the time that the counseling and coaching I was receiving from her would help me deal with the adversity of going through a divorce, losing a house and a job at the same time, and raising two children on a shoe string.

Jean still works with me today. The focus of our meetings is how to remain spiritually centered in all areas of my life. We go over concepts that are applicable to whatever is going on in my life. She provides for me an outside perspective to things I could easily get obsessed about. Her major contribution during the time of turbulence was to let me know that God still loved me and believed in me if I would believe in Him.

The other people are Stan Blinkhorn and Don and Carol Cassetty. These individuals were responsible for helping me find friends when I needed help financially. It is really difficult to find financial assistance when everything has fallen out from under you. Once, Stan said, "It's not how much you don't have, it's how much you still have." I was down to $300, or, as he'd put it, "You still HAVE $300." The idea is to work from a position of abundance rather than a position of scarcity. Those of us who have received help financially know the challenge of maintaining our dignity. Don, Carol and Stan knew of my capabilities and were confident that I could again run a household effectively.

Finally, Harvey Booth, my friend and pastor at Cedar Hills Baptist Church, prayed with me and bought my groceries once. He would take me to the store for a coke. He kept telling me, "You will be bigger than you were before."

All of us need to know that there are people who believe in us. There are many who love us, but sometimes they make inappropriate remarks or try to help in ways that are not useful at the time. I think managers of work groups and coaches of sports teams convey belief in their players. They know it, too. How many times do you see a team with lots of talent not win the championship? It is a matter of providing the right kind of support at the right moment.

A friend and former classmate, Jim Manary, once said, "When you are trying to decide how much time to commit to church activities it may be wise to give five percent of your time and go all the way with the commitments you have instead of committing yourself ten percent of the time and not following through with what you signed up for." I have never forgotten that remark. Don, Carol, Stan, and Harvey were with me during the darkest days of my life. In some cases, they went with me to help obtain the needed money or resources. Sometimes they even spoke with others on my behalf.

My part during this time in life was to allow others to serve me and to help them help me. I made a commitment on how I would pay people back. I worked hard to be gracious for the help I received and I had a renewed faith that I could succeed and build a real business. When I work with individuals and organizations, I strive to let them know that anything is possible. I do believe that. I now believe that God could give me eyesight, but I no longer resent Him because He hasn't done that. He has a purpose for my life the way I am. I have learned about joy and peace and love. You do not have to be sighted to have those qualities.

There is nothing wrong with making specific requests. God has answered all of my requests and in most cases I got what I asked Him for.

When we have established our belief in God, then we must pray and wait expectantly. We need to create a vision of what we want to do and then vision ourselves as already having accomplished that vision before it actually happens.

When my oldest son was eighteen months old, I tried an experiment. We went out for a walk on a cold, raining night. Both of us were dressed for the weather. I wanted to see how Erik would follow my instructions as we walked. I would hold my cane in my right hand and his hand in my left. I don't know what happened, but I accidentally dropped my cane. I then said to him, "Erik, Daddy has dropped his cane. I need you to walk over and find it, pick it up, and bring it back to me." As I let go of his hand, I wasn't sure what he was going to do. What I did, however, was convey to him that he would walk over and get it, bring it back, and hand it right to me. He did have other options (like walking out in the middle of the street, playing in the bushes, or play hide and seek.)

Erik walked over to the cane, picked it up, and brought it right back to me. He seemed to know the seriousness of my command. He responded to my expectations that he would do what I wanted him to.

He seemed to know the difference between when to play and when to respond in the way that he did.

During the same eighteen-month period, Erik seemed to know when it was okay to play around. One time I was trying to find him to punish him. He was sitting on the table and not breathing. The goal for him was to trick me. I knew he was around somewhere. Eventually he breathed, and I pounced. Employees or older children know when parents or managers expect them to produce. We convey an attitude as leaders that we know they can do it.

The challenge comes when our subordinates are not doing well. Their life is a mess, and still we must deal with the present situation while at the same time conveying to them that eventually they can get themselves back on their feet. My friends knew I would eventually become successful. It didn't happen overnight. They and I expected to see me back in the workforce providing a strong contribution financially to my family.

Once we believe and expect, then we must wait for God's answer. My wife, Becky, says that there are two kinds of waiting, the first kind is to be still. Psalms 46:10 says, "Be still and know that I am God." We listen for God's leading, or some unexpected thing to happen, and that serves as his response or an answer to our prayer.

God answers requests in the most unexpected ways and at the most unexpected times. Many people think that if they pray and do nothing that God will still give them what you want. That is not always true. Faith without work is not faith.

The second kind of waiting is in the form of action. It may come in the form of asking questions, requesting that others pray for you, and conducting research about the things we are praying for. Becky says that this kind of waiting may also come in the form of serving others. The people who are waiting on us are serving us.

When my first marriage was dissolving, I had to move the boys into a two-bedroom apartment. I also became the president of my professional organization. I was serving my profession. The real truth is that in serving others, I got more out of it than they did. It may be hard for some of us to have a servant's mentality when other parts of your world are caving in around us.

Today I work to convey to all people that I have faith in them. I want them to know that I believe in them when they do not believe in themselves. I want them to create a vision for themselves and expect that they can get there. I then coach them to take action and then wait. I guess when push comes to shove, I don't exactly know how this faith thing works either, but I do know it is exciting and reassuring to know that it does work. We learn to develop a divine perspective on the ordinary side of life. Live from faith and do it expectantly.

CHAPTER 10

A Call to Service

SHE IS THE FIRST ASIAN TEACHER AT THE California School for the Blind. She is teaching second grade. The superintendent walks into her classroom. "Miss Tekawa," he begins, "I'm sending a Japanese boy to you. As you know, students must read and write Braille before they advance to the second grade. He can do neither, though he has been with us three years — two in the first grade and one in kindergarten."

"What do you want me to do?" she inquires

"I don't know," he replies. "But do something."

For four months she watches. She observes he "broadcasts" baseball games, seems adept with statistics, and has an excellent memory. One day she says, "Stephen, to be a radio announcer, you must learn Braille so you can read commercials and players' batting averages. Knowing Braille will help you be a good play-by-play person."

"I could be a radio announcer if I learn Braille?" he asks.

"Yes. But only if you learn Braille."

She introduces him to whole words instead of the alphabet. His first word in Braille is "ball," the next "run," then "hit," then "to the base."

I was spellbound when I heard this story being told at a class reunion at the California School for the Blind. It explained so much. Miss Tekawa had used baseball to motivate me to learn Braille. I had moved from the bottom of the class to the top of the class within three months.

The reunion was the first gathering of our group of students since we left the school. We caught up with one another and described what it had meant to us to become successful.

Our goals in the school had been to graduate, meet a sighted person, marry her, and get a job. Each person at the table had accomplished that and more. If only twenty-one percent of the blind population is employed nationally today, then I had been in an exceptional group in an exceptional school.

This reunion was timely because I had been dealing with challenges both in my consulting firm and the business, a town car service, I had started. That evening, the definition the others and I placed on success served as a reminder that we were living life just like everyone else, whether blind or sighted.

In those days our goal was to assimilate into mainstream society, to be like the American "norm."

I think that is why diversity is so important to me today and why I find it so rewarding to help people feel good about who they are as individuals. We are all different. Still, we dream about succeeding financially, emotionally, and spiritually.

I feel that I succeed if I move steadily toward my goal on a daily basis. Our benchmarks for success are measured by our vision of what we want to become in life.

I never would have thought in those days at the School for the Blind that it was possible to meet someone, get married, have a job, and then to start two businesses. It became clear to me that night at the reunion that no one succeeds without help from others. Some of us need help more often, but we can contribute if we have developed skills. Had I not learned how to read or write Braille, I would be stuck today.

I would not have the ability to keep track of things. I have yet to broadcast an inning of baseball, but I have been able to speak to thousands of people around the United States. I have helped organizations transform themselves into something they didn't think was possible.

All of us at the School for the Blind knew pain, doubt and fear, but we also had a staff committed to serving us and helping us succeed. The call to servanthood was alive inside them. I am thankful that I can see the fruits of their labor. No longer need I feel bad about my condition.

There are eight stages of development in life. Knowing them may help us understand what might be happening to people we work with who are different from us. These stages may also help us understand where we are in the process.

The first developmental stage is discovery. The discovery that we are different can be frightening, unsettling, or exciting.

In my workshops, I have had African-Americans who while in the South attended all-black schools during the 1950s and 1960s. When they moved to the North, they walked into all-white classrooms. "Where are the other black students?" they wondered.

I was walking down the street at the age of four with Mom and Aunt Chiz.

"There's a dog," I said, pointing. Mom and Aunt Chiz went wild!

"He can see! He can see!" they exclaimed.

I could see only shadows, but I thought that was the way it was for everyone. Eventually, I learned that I could not see and that as a result I would have to go away to a school. This was when I discovered that I was different from other children.

Often, difference seems to mean there is something wrong about the person, about his or her approach, or about a situation itself. The mountain to climb to success may be more difficult if we are different. It shouldn't be, but it is.

The second developmental stage is anger. Anger is often a response to unfairness. It didn't seem to me that it was fair that I was blind. It isn't fair when someone gets cancer. It isn't fair when one person has more power than another. It is this latter category that has created conflict in this world.

Wars between races, generations, and countries have been set off by issues of rights, privileges, and power.

When something makes me angry, I do something about it immediately. If someone hits me, I hit them back. That's how we resolved our anger as children. We demonstrated our manhood or strength.

Resolution of anger becomes more difficult when groups of people are impacted by acts of wrongdoing, like the Oklahoma City bombing. Justice is different from fairness.

The goal of justice is to catch the person who committed a crime and bring that person to justice to suffer the consequences of his or her acts. Those who have lost loved ones view the terrible act as unfair. Women and minorities in this country become angry when jobs are not given to them once they have achieved the level of competency required to do the work. As one who has experienced discrimination or the feeling of being weak, I want the opportunity to do what I can do based on my competencies.

The third stage of development is doubt. Doubt precludes confidence. Doubt can arise from a need for approval, the need for safety, or the need to belong. Comments from others, as well as the belief that I am inadequate or incapable, can send me into serious doubt. During this phase, I don't allow my talents to come to the forefront.

Doubt also precludes belief. This can contribute to the erosion of relationships, even when two people love each other.

A child dreams of doing something. Well-meaning parents

might say, "Don't do that; you must do math; there's not enough money; that's impossible." The parents are trying to protect their children from being hurt when, in fact, the hurt that the child experiences may be part of the learning process.

This can be a difficult challenge for parents whose children have disabilities. A good manager or parent learns to convey belief in the individual while still redirecting the individual's effort or picture of their situation.

Certainly, my second grade teacher found a way to convey belief in me. It surpassed any doubt I had about learning Braille. Doubt is the stage where we feel scattered, fragmented, and not good about ourselves.

The fourth stage is seclusion, which is marked initially by withdrawal. I was the world's best. I withdrew so I could escape facing conflict and pain. I hoped the problem would go away.

Seclusion, in its worst form, means we resign and are not present with others. Often, keeping busy is a form of seclusion we use while we mask our true feelings.

Another form of seclusion, however, is to retreat and regroup or get ourselves together so we can deal with our problems later. This kind of seclusion is more of a retreat or restoring of oneself.

Since I have been studying God's Word, I find that it is necessary to go into seclusion to restore myself. I spend time daily in scripture and prayer. During this time, I remove myself from my daily circumstances long enough to obtain perspective and to experience joy or peace. This does not mean I avoid my problems or that I am always successful.

These two forms of seclusion are very different. I find that one has an adverse effect on me, while the other is very positive. There are not many people who know themselves well enough to determine the form of seclusion in which they are engaged.

While a boy, I decided to numb myself from the pain of leaving home. By numbing myself, I endured the pain, but I also missed out on experiencing authentic relationships that I thought were not possible to have. I am continually amazed at the resilience of the human condition, which learns coping mechanisms to help us do what we need to do. Sometimes we could do better, but we do not yet know how or have not yet been properly equipped to handle a variety of situations.

Many people in the workplace are in seclusion.

Despair is another form of seclusion. An individual may need to seek clinical help. While working at the Oregon Commission for the Blind as Director of the Rehabilitation Center, I heard many people describe what it was like to lose their sight. Some reported closing their blinds for an entire year, thus shutting themselves away from the rest of the world while they dealt with their grief.

One way to help someone get out of this type of seclusion is to "love them back to health." This effort requires a commitment to demonstrate to people that we believe in them when they don't believe in themselves. We must stay with them and help them get into action.

The fifth stage of development is rebirth.

Fritz Perls said it is painful to die and be born again. John C. Maxwell believed the bigger the problem, the bigger the opportunity. I like imagining that when one door closes, another opens.

All of these sayings get at the same thing. When there is a death in a relationship, there is reason to believe in newness. In fact, as each day comes to an end, we have an opportunity to create new beginnings. If a tragedy strikes, we may need to adjust how those new beginnings are created. God has made it possible for us to begin anew each day. I did not know this during those days at the School for the Blind.

When my first marriage dissolved, I was in a different place in my life. I could see new possibilities, though I didn't know yet what they were. The year following my divorce, I traveled to Hawaii. Unexpectedly, I began to learn how to become more dependent and independent at the same time.

Perhaps the true rebirth is internal. It may mean giving up a particular way of thinking, stopping a bad habit, or changing ideas regarding a particular person. Rebirth is a byproduct of the form of seclusion in which we go away and restore ourselves by reading, resting, swimming, or vacationing. It may also mean we start our lives again in terms of relationships. Sometimes it means we leave old relationships or reframe relationships we are presently in. Reframing is more difficult to pull off.

Rebirth can also be celebrated in nature. I come alive

again when I am outside listening to birds and walking on a trail.

We can celebrate accomplishments — ours or those of others — if we take care not to forget God, the source of our help. I love comeback stories in which an injured athlete overcomes incredible odds to regain his or her original playing capability.

I find that my life is constantly emerging and that I am learning new things daily about how to be with others and myself. That is what is so wondrous about the journey. There are always new possibilities to develop.

The sixth developmental stage is the need to belong. I was sitting in a Japanese thought-pattern class a few years ago, listening to the instructor tell about different ways American and Japanese parents discipline their children. In the Japanese culture, when children do something wrong, they are told to leave the house or go outside. In American culture, the children are grounded or sent to their rooms.

A light bulb turned on in my head. I remembered being told to sleep on the porch when I did something wrong. My brother was locked out of the house if he got home late. My upbringing was American, yet my father retained some Japanese methodology for discipline. The need to belong is so strong in the Japanese culture that if we are kicked out, thrown out, or asked to leave, we feel excluded, and we feel bad.

When Neil was twelve, he had a slumber party. Twelve boys stayed the night. Little did we realize once we went to bed that the night had only begun. Two boys went out to buy eggs, and then ten boys "egged" the neighborhood. We had moved in only six months earlier. Not until two days after the slumber party did we learn about the "egging." One boy did not take part, but he did not tell us about it either. Neil himself did not take part but kept it secret. What drove these two boys not to tell us? Was it the need to belong?

As a parent, I understood the need. I wanted to belong to the neighborhood. I wanted to be known as a respectable member. I felt an incredible sense of embarrassment for what the boys did. Becky and I called the parents and asked that each boy come back and apologize to the neighbors.

I think the need to belong is so strong that sometimes we give away our individuality or it is taken from us. We make choices we regret.

The need to belong should be strong enough to give us a sense of value and worth. The value must be driven from a perspective of Christlike love, which allows people to be who they are and assists others to learn how to accept God's direction for our life.

I have spent so much time trying to belong that I haven't devoted enough time to who I am. I am getting better now at bringing myself forward. I have a real sense of belonging to different groups. I am privileged to belong to a group of people who go out to lunch after church on Sunday. I belong to a group of consultants who respect me. I belong to a family who loves me even when they don't always like what I do. I am also keenly aware that many others do not have this.

The dilemma comes when we try to act on our own without first seeking counsel from Him.

The seventh developmental stage is that of the con artist, who struggles with the moment of truth and who acts as if all is okay when it is not.

I think back on the time we blind children tried to convince ourselves we could see. We could not accept hanging on to someone's arm to go "sighted guide" (a term describing how sighted people lead blind people.) Instead, we would walk down the street, brushing each other's arm occasionally for guidance. The goal was to look sighted. We thought we were pretty cool.

We thought we looked like normal sighted boys until one day my friend suddenly fell into an open utility hole. Oddly enough, my friend was not concerned about what had gone wrong or how he had been nearly hurt when he tried to pretend he was sighted. The only thing that upset him was losing his ice cream cone.

During the early days of Equal Employment Opportunity and Affirmative Action, organizations felt forced to hire women and minorities. EEO and AA are criticized today by organizations that feel they must lower workplace standards in order to comply with these regulations. This criticism makes the assumption that women and minorities may not be the most qualified people for the job.

The con-artist behavior comes when organizations and employees act as if all is okay when it is not. The struggle for the con artist is to face what is true.

The truth for the students in the School for the Blind was that no matter how we tried, we would not be sighted. We had to understand that and yet still have positive self-esteem for ourselves as we were.

The truth for an employer is to face the fact that there are qualified women and minorities that can do the job.

Con artists need to acknowledge that they are out of alignment with themselves and with others. The con artist needs to be encouraged, to believe in empowerment, and to become properly equipped. Those who are con artists act like they are something they are not.

How does this differ from visualizing a goal? In striving to reach a goal, we are clear about the resources we have, the resources we need, and about enlisting help from others.

The eighth developmental stage is self-actualization. This is the time in life when things begin to come together. We know our strengths and weaknesses and, more importantly, we begin to be at peace with them.

When I first thought about writing this portion of the book, I considered it a surface discussion about becoming comfortable with ourselves, faults and all.

However, within the past few years, I have come to realize that the walk with God and being in the Holy Spirit are crucial to the self-actualization process. I mean that the energy flow becomes more fluid and effortless and the challenges, responsibilities, and opportunities are greater.

I heard a sermon not too long ago by Derrick Johnson, who talked about the importance of understanding that God sees us when we don't see Him. He is never late. He may allow us to experience the storm before He takes us out of it. As Johnson talked about the disciples leaving the place where Jesus had fed five-thousand, he said that God had needed to get the disciples to move out of their comfort zone because they had become complacent. We can become complacent with how things are in the world.

When I turned fifty, I thought life should be a little easier. Suddenly, I was experiencing business difficulties again. Cash flow was getting tight. Just as God moved the disciples out of their comfort zone, so had He moved me out of mine. He was testing my faith. I didn't know it then, but I do now.

I had become too comfortable with my newfound success — success that I never could have conceived during those years at the School for the Blind. Sitting at the table during the class reunion brought it all together. The journey is complete now, though it is not over.

Self-actualization is that time in life when we know how to address adversity, when we have skills for dealing with life's glitches. We also become open to the joy, love, and happiness that are ours to experience. I feel ready to take on what God wants me to do. Everything I have been writing about to this point has been preparation.

He had to do a significant amount of work in me, as He does with you. He has had to work with me to tear down my bitterness, fear, doubt, and anxiety. I continue to experience these emotions, but what is different today is that I know how to redirect myself.

I also have come to grips with my own weaknesses. When I began writing this book I wanted you to know how I had overcome obstacles, conquered the odds, and made a success of my life. As I sit here writing about self-actualization, I now know that the weaker I am, the stronger I can be. The point is that I no longer have to do things by myself.

Sometimes I come home from a workshop and wonder how I was able to get a group to "move" or to begin a change process. The answer is that I didn't get them to move or shift; the Holy Spirit was moving through me and did the work. I was merely a way station for the information that needed to reach its intended audience. The thing I have learned about doing workshops is that I can do my best and still not succeed if the audience is unwilling to participate.

Once I gave a presentation before an executive staff of a high tech firm. If successful in my presentation, I would be conducting a series of workshops for more than eight-hundred people in the division. As I began my presentation, I could sense that the management team did not like the work. I had to convince them every step of the way why this project was important or why this workplace culture liked to do something in this way. A colleague said it was the best work she'd seen from me, but that the people were not ready to hear the message. Someone once said, "When the students are ready, the teacher will appear." The students were not ready in this case.

I am now learning how to be mad, sad, and glad, and to enjoy life. I wish I could run by myself, drive a car, or see the faces of my family. The emotions I feel when I wish for these things are temporary now. No longer do I experience rage or resentment at being blind.

I am the creator of any business or family venture I choose to take part in, and God is always my senior partner.

Each of us has the opportunity to have a similar relationship. The activities we engage in are based on who we are and what we are called to do in the world. There are trials and tribulations, and I face them, as do most of us.

I appreciate and value my success. I have received affirmation from family, friends, and colleagues. This makes life easier to handle when adversity arises.

There are seven statements that have helped me understand what it means to have a positive handle on self-actualization. These statements come from Pastor Ron Mehl of Beaverton Four Square Church in Beaverton, Oregon.

1. God is good.

2. God is just.

3. God is powerful.

4. He never lets you have a problem beyond your ability to deal with it.

5. God is always on time.

6. He has a purpose larger than yourself or your own goals.

7. God cares.

I can truly attest to the fact that these seven points have been pertinent to a variety of situations in my life. I am clear now that He has a bigger purpose in which I am to be involved just as I am. My blindness reminds me that we all need help from one another. My speaking ability and my ethnicity easily identify me to others. My role is to take responsibility for these gifts and to provide the people I come in contact with something they can take away for themselves. The credit goes to God. That's hard for me to see sometimes because I like affirmation. I am slowly learning that I don't need accolades as much as I thought I did.

Once self-understanding and self-acceptance begin to take place, we can look at how to triple the work we are called to do.

We can do this because we are clear about who we are and what is important to us. In my own case, I have a mission for my business and for myself personally.

Secondly, I have values that are important for me to live by. The mission drives the choices I make for myself and the world in which I live.

The times I have felt the best about myself are when I am doing something for someone else. I believe that we need to focus on becoming people of influence. This influence comes in the form of service, leadership, and making a difference in the lives of others.

Here are some steps I recommend to increase our ability

to serve and lead others. First, we need to watch and listen to what others say and do. In some instances, we may also need to listen for what is not said. We need to take note of who does what to influence the environment we are in.

Second, we need to develop our surrendering skills. This means that we learn the importance of following people and principles that are important to us. We will call on them in difficult situations. Following, surrendering, and submitting should not be confused with resignation. I surrender to an awesome God and through Him the energy flows. I get direction for how to live my life, who to be around, and also how to refine and develop the gifts and talents I have been given.

Third, we need to develop a solid plan for self-discipline. Only within the last two to three years have I been able to work on discipline in all areas of my life. Spiritually I work to read scripture twice daily. Some days I read it more often than others. It is important to seek counsel, guidance, and knowledge from God's Word.

Physically I work out on my treadmill or by running with friends. When I travel, I ask for a hotel that has room service and a workout facility. It is not always possible to get my physical workout in, but I still strive to make that a very important part of my travel itinerary.

Emotionally, I find it helpful to work continually on cultivating healthy relationships. We need to make it a practice to connect with someone who really affirms us for who we are on a regular basis. This does not mean we have heavy discussions about what is happening in our lives. Sometimes we connect only for a cup of coffee or a run.

What we are really talking about here is the need to work on balance in our lives. This is increasingly difficult in this age when it is possible always to be in demand for work-related concerns.

The fourth step to helping increase our ability to serve others is to see the goal. I am intrigued by how much time and money are spent helping organizations work on strategic planning. Before we can plan, we must have a vision. From the vision, we develop goals. Next, we create plans that put the goals into operation.

I think there is only one goal in life. That is to be as Christlike as possible. Many nonbelievers say that they are not into organized religion. That is not what I'm talking about. To be Christlike means that I develop a relationship with Him. I learn to be kind, loving, compassionate, and understanding. I adopt standards and principles I live by out of love, not out of law or doctrine.

In Galatians, we learn that Jesus redeemed us from the law. What that means to me is that by forgiving error, we encourage people who are "down," and we become providers of strength and leadership to those in need.

We do not have to be parrots or robots in order to be Christlike. Because of who we are, we come into contact with people different from ourselves. We listen for God's lead.

Finally, we take responsibility. We take responsibility for

our gifts and talents. If we are managers, leaders, or coaches, we take responsibility for creating an environment so that the people who report to us can use their unique gifts and talents. Many of my colleagues in diversity talk about helping the oppressed. That is a biblical concept.

The emphasis should be on helping people develop and use the gifts they have been given. We have devoted too much time to trying to make everyone in the world equal.

We can assist people beyond what they believe is possible when we embrace the characteristics of Christlikeness and not churchlikeness drawn from a doctrinal stand. The church is important to me for purposes of fellowship, encouragement, and worship. Since humans staff the church, it can also be an imperfect entity on occasion. We need to help our nonbelieving brothers and sisters understand our humanness.

I once downplayed my gifts. When we have a gift to share, there is much glory to be gained, but we are also open to criticism. As a person who wanted and needed approval and who did not like conflict, I found it easier not to take responsibility for what I can do. Today I still want to be needed and valued. I still want to avoid conflict, but now I see the necessity to respond to what I am called to do and be.

I am called to serve others. Success on an external basis is not all that it's cracked up to be. With it comes responsibility and the fear of pressure as others want more from us. When the success we seek becomes internalized and an integral part of who we are, it is easier to maintain balance and focus.

Perhaps preaching about servanthood cannot begin to make a difference until we know what it is like to be served by others. I have been served by so many people that I understand it is through others that I become a more fulfilled human being. The journey is to become as Christlike as possible.

I have found joy. I know who I am, what it took to get where I am, and what it is going to take to continue the process of giving to others. The journey is far from over.

About the Author:

STEVE HANAMURA is founder and co-owner of Hanamura Consulting, Inc. Steve brings over 30 years experience to the consulting, training and speaking profession. He is widely sought after in the areas of leadership development, managing and leading diversity initiatives, building effective teams and managing personal and organizational change.

Steve is listed in Who's Who in Executives and Professionals and is a member of the Diversity Collegium (A think tank of Diversity professionals). He was chair of the board for the Oregon Commission for the Blind from 1991–1997. Among his honors are the American Society for Training and Development Multicultural Network Trainer of the Year award as well as his selection as one of the Tourchbearers for the 1996 Olympics.